SELF-CARE FOR ECO-ANXIETY

To all who love Mother Earth,
She loves you too.

SELF-CARE FOR ECO-ANXIETY

**52 Weekly Practices for
Positive, Personal Change
Through the Power of Nature**

Hardie Grant

BOOKS

Rachael Cohen

CONTENTS

Earth is not dying.

Introduction

Despite all you see in the news, despite the real and scary changes we're already witnessing across the globe, Earth herself is very much alive.

What is on the brink of demise, though, is the comfortable environment and seemingly unlimited resources we humans have benefited from, and unfortunately taken for granted, for centuries. Earth is not dying, but the way of life that made Earth comfortable and enjoyable for people (and lots of other species) appears to be dying right in front of us.

The worst part of it is that this way of life here on Earth is dying at our own hands. Well, not you and me specifically, but by the hands of the governing, economic and industrial systems humans created and continue to maintain.

This fact is equally infuriating, frightening and heartbreaking.

Infuriating because we know there are more harmonious and life-affirming ways to live on this biodiverse and beautiful planet. Frightening because the impacts of climate change, habitat destruction, pollution and constant consumption are already being felt around the globe and are only projected to get worse. And heartbreaking because we are grieving the loss of life, biodiversity, habitats, health, and so much more.

If you feel anxious, angry, depressed and disempowered about climate change as well as the damage being done to Earth and all that live upon her, please know you are not alone. In fact, this dread and dismay over humanity's destruction of Earth is so prevalent, it's now got its own name: eco-anxiety.

Please know you are not alone.

Eco-Anxiety:
What it is and Why it Matters

According to the American Psychological Association, eco-anxiety is the 'chronic fear of environmental doom' and it's a feeling that is now pervasive for millions. While not an official medical diagnosis, eco-anxiety encompasses feelings of fear, anger, sadness, guilt, stress, disempowerment, depression and grief due to climate change and the destruction of the natural world.

As with other forms of anxiety and depression, eco-anxiety manifests in varying ways and degrees of severity. From spiralling, repetitive thoughts that make focus, conversation and sleep difficult, to hypervigilance and feelings of guilt over our footprint on the Earth, to anger over the lack of urgency from world leaders, to sadness and disempowerment over our perceived lack of control and influence. I believe our feelings of eco-anxiety also speak to a truth we're currently not discussing nearly enough. The truth that we humans are not separate from the planet we live on. The truth that we cannot separate our health from the health of the planet.

When we pollute the air, the water and the soil, we degrade the very air, water and food we ingest. When we continue to burn fossil fuels, even as we feel the impacts of climate change all around, we sacrifice future opportunities for today's convenience. When we lose species and habitats, we lose some of our own wild and embodied nature. Is it any wonder we feel anxious? Enraged? Frustrated? Overwhelmed? Confused? Sad?

Feelings of eco-anxiety are a perfectly sane response to a society that is acting in an insane way. Our feelings of anxiety, fear, anger, frustration, sadness, dismay and grief are natural and valid responses to the reality of the situations at hand.

And yet...

The intense feelings brought on by eco-anxiety can prevent us appreciating the beauty of the natural world, as well as rob us of the connections and possibilities that are still alive all around us.

Even as we despair about the state of the world, Earth still exists in a state of awe-inspiring beauty and interdependence. The Sun and Moon still rise and set, leaves change colour as seasons pass, while some are born and others die. Life is always adapting, persisting and living on.

When we worry and stress over the impacts of climate change and environmental destruction, to the point of negatively impacting our mental health, we end up feeling resigned, fearful and depressed over the environmental crisis we face. We also forget that solutions to this crisis are readily available, just waiting to be implemented. We forget that there are already millions around the globe, like you and I, who care about the Earth and take daily actions to protect the planet. We deny ourselves the visionary power of hope.

Hope matters.

The way we feel matters as we attempt to meet the environmental challenges we currently face. Our fear, guilt, sadness and anxiety have not inspired the changes we need. If anything, our feelings of eco-anxiety keep us feeling disempowered and resigned to the status quo.

Feelings of eco-anxiety are a perfectly sane response to a society that is acting in an insane way. Our feelings of anxiety, fear, anger, frustration, sadness, dismay and grief are natural and valid responses to the reality of the situations at hand.

Fear and the 'doom and gloom' approach to climate and environmental catastrophes aren't motivating us to create a more sustainable way of living upon Earth. Yet I believe love will. Love for Earth, ourselves and the many species that call Earth home.

That's what this book is all about: returning to a sense of love and connection with Earth, through Nature-based self-care practices that combat the fear, guilt and disempowerment caused by eco-anxiety.

This book is not about the solutions to climate change, although inspiring solutions are shared. This is also not a book about minimising your environmental footprint, although there are practices in the book that will help you do just that. This book is about taking care of yourself, your mental health, your sense of connection and your hope for the future through a loving relationship with Nature. This book is here to create solutions, resilience and change within you. Because all true lasting change starts from within.

This book encourages inner change, which helps us to heal and care for ourselves while caring for Nature, too. When we heal, Earth heals; just as when Earth heals, we heal. Our feelings of anxiety, guilt and sadness over the damage to Earth can be transformed into connection, creativity and inspired action. From that place we can create lasting change and feel much happier, as well as more purposeful and powerful in our lives. Our healing, just like our living, is symbiotic with that of the Earth.

And I know this to be true because of my own experience with eco-anxiety. As a child, I felt a spark of divine connection while climbing trees, exploring creeks and playing in the ocean. The natural world always gave me a feeling of belonging to something bigger, brighter and more loving.

I dedicated my career to sharing humanity's interconnectivity with Earth. This brought me to Hawaii, where I taught ocean conservation and studied dolphins and whales. Later, I took care of wild animals at the San Diego Zoo, teaching visitors about their natural habitats. Next, I earned a Master's degree and landed my dream job at the Monterey Bay Aquarium.

I was living in my purpose, connecting

Nature has the power to inspire and maintain well-being, but only if we allow it.

people with Nature, yet I was also on anti-anxiety medications and sleeping pills to deal with my ever-present dread. I was in deep with eco-anxiety. The more I learned about the challenges facing the ocean, climate and planet, the more afraid I became. Even teaching about solutions made me spiral, because it was clear that society wasn't willing to protect Earth or her inhabitants.

Medication and therapy helped me bury these intense feelings of eco-anxiety. Working for organisations dedicated to preserving life on Earth also helped. Then I became a mother, and my fear about the future intensified. After my second daughter was born, my eco-anxiety grew to the point where I could barely sleep or eat, and I lost my joy for living. I found myself denying Nature's beauty. Earth still appeared beautiful on the surface, yet when I looked deeper, all I saw were her wounds. I was cut off from hope.

Then a creative relationship with plants changed everything.

My therapist suggested I get creative, so while my children napped, I immersed myself in Nature by creating plant art with succulents. My ruminating thoughts fell silent and my aching heart unclenched. I felt fully present to the beauty of the plants, soil, stones and my own creativity. In this place of presence, hands in soil and fingers stroking leaves, I was reminded that life, beauty and interdependence surround us. I realised I had a choice. I could constantly focus on environmental destruction, or I could focus on Earth's inspirational beauty, function and a more sustainable future. I chose the latter.

This creative and personal relationship with plants reconnected me with Nature in ways that my soul longed for. I remembered my spiritual connection and leaned into Earth's reciprocal love.

This is how I began my plant art, styling and, eventually, life coaching business. As Nature helped me heal through creativity and deeper connection, I was guided to help others do the same.

Nature has the power to inspire and maintain well-being, but only if we allow it. Even now, when I feel surges of sadness, fear and guilt over our treatment of Earth, I go to Nature. I connect, create and give back from a place of love.

And in the pages to come I guide you to do the same.

How to Use this Book

Throughout the pages of this book, you'll learn 52 self-care practices to ease your eco-anxiety and reconnect you with a loving relationship with Nature. The self-care practices are organised into three themes: connecting with Nature, creating with Nature and giving back to Nature.

The self-care practices build off each other and are meant to be read and applied consecutively at first. Yet you, dear reader, are free to pick and choose the practices you wish and that suit your needs. I do suggest that you partake in the Nature connection and Nature creativity sections prior to conducting any giving back to Nature practices. This will ensure you are taking action for Earth from a place of connection, gratitude and love.

These practices are meant to be adapted and evolved through you and your personal practice. You'll find space to reflect upon many of the self-care practices, helping you determine the ones that bring you the most benefit. Please do not use this book as another 'to-do list' or way to shame yourself for not doing enough. The self-care practices are about connection, well-being and belief in a better future, and are not meant to bring any additional guilt or shame into your life.

52 SELF-CARE PRACTICES FOR ECO-ANXIETY

'Look deep into
Nature, and then
you will understand
everything better.'

— Albert Einstein

Time spent in Nature is good for us
physically, mentally and emotionally.
We feel better after being in natural
spaces. Yet too often we fail to connect
with the Nature all around us, while
complaining about how disconnected
we feel. While getting out into the
wilderness is fantastic, it's not necessary
for re-engaging with Nature. From the
birds and the clouds in the sky, to the
grass and the ants at our feet, Nature
is always around us, just waiting for
our reconnection. The following self-
care practices focus on connecting with
Nature through your own awareness –
body, mind and soul.

CONNECT
WITH
NATURE

Wake Up with Nature

The natural progression of our brain upon waking is to go from dreamy delta waves into sleepy yet aware theta waves, then awake and relaxed alpha waves before moving into the beta state of awake, alert and focused. This natural progression provides us with time to be more present with ourselves and our subconscious – that part of us that we often keep hidden from others and yet is home to our beliefs and sense of self. The theta and alpha states in particular help us connect with ourselves and the world immediately around us in creative and receptive ways.

When we immerse ourselves in screens first thing in the morning, we force our brain to go from dreamy delta into the analysing and focused beta state, skipping over the benefits of the theta and alpha waves. We let in stressors, pressures and dramas before we even have a moment to connect with ourselves. Instead, when you wake up, spend time present with Nature before going on your phone, computer or television. Instead of grabbing your phone as soon as you wake up, try the following first:

1. Spend time with plants. This could entail spending time wiping down and checking the soil moisture of your houseplants, checking the growth in your garden or simply staring at greenery from your window as you sip on some tea or coffee. Notice the different shades and textures, and the way the light and shadows play off the leaves. Just breathe and be present.

2. Spend a few minutes stretching your body in any way that feels good for you, as you intentionally connect with the Earth beneath your feet and the Sun above your head. As you move and enjoy the flowing movement

of your body, breathe deeply and intentionally, imagining yourself pulling in nourishment from the Earth and energy from the Sun. While this practice can be done anywhere, it feels especially wonderful outdoors.

3 Spend a few minutes thinking about or interacting with loved ones – including pets – appreciating their presence in your life.

4 Spend time journalling in the morning, a practice described in the book *The Artist's Way* by Julia Cameron as 'morning pages'. Each morning, journal for three pages in a stream of consciousness. What you write doesn't matter at all, just let yourself note down whatever wants to come out of you. Remember, spending time with yourself is spending time with Nature, because you are Nature too.

**SPEND TIME PRESENT WITH NATURE
BEFORE GOING ON YOUR PHONE,
COMPUTER OR TELEVISION.**

Nature and the Nervous System

Eco-anxiety is wreaking havoc on our nervous systems as we spiral through feelings of rage (fight), fear (flight), disempowerment (fawn) and depression (freeze).

The nervous system connects our body to our brain, and our brain to our body. It's responsible for how we function, physically, emotionally and mentally – both consciously and subconsciously. Among many other functions, our nervous system governs our breath, heart rate, digestion and sleep, along with our thoughts and emotions. The sympathetic system governs our ability to motivate ourselves and take action, while also spurring us to fight or flee when faced with a perceived threat. The parasympathetic system governs our ability to rest, relax, sleep and digest, while also making us fawn (people please), freeze or fully collapse, when we feel unsafe.

Nature positively influences our nervous system by helping us move from the stress response of our sympathetic nervous system into the relaxation response of our parasympathetic system. Yet as we continue to worry and grieve over our current treatment of Earth, we turn that which was once our respite from daily stressors into another source of suffering and chronic stress. The solutions and creativity needed to remedy our environmental situation cannot be accessed when we as a collective are stuck in fight, flight, fawn or freeze.

Thankfully, there are somatic practices that help regulate our nervous systems. Somatics are body-led practices that use the mind-body connection to communicate with our inner sensations and emotions. Somatic practices help us release the weight of old emotional baggage, while accessing safety and pleasure within. Somatic practices are self-care practices. When we pair these with exposure to Nature, we create powerful moments of inner acceptance and transformation.

The following
Nature-based somatic
self-care practices are
designed to help you move
through feelings of fight,
flight, fawn and freeze,
in order to return to
a sense of safety within
yourself and on Earth.

Let Go of Anger

The anger and rage we feel about environmental destruction is valid, yet holding this anger inside dysregulates our nervous system and keeps us feeling stressed. The following somatic practice releases rage in healthy ways, using awareness of the body and help from Mother Earth. Also, please don't feel guilty or bad for releasing your rage into Earth. Think of these practices as emotional composting – where we release our emotional waste into Earth, knowing she will transform it back into material for growth!

1. Find a secluded spot outdoors where you will not be disturbed. Sitting or lying on the ground, allow yourself to truly feel the anger you hold inside regarding climate change and environmental abuse. Don't rationalise or repress the anger. Begin to shake your head as if you're saying no, while you kick or stomp your feet and (gently) beat your fists on the ground. Let yourself have a temper tantrum in order to let that anger move through you! Keep hitting, kicking and shaking your head until you feel the anger dissipate and a sense of quietness, or calm, settle within you.

2. With your face pressed to the Earth or into a pillow, scream as loudly as you can, shouting out your anger, frustration and rage. Keep this up until you feel calm again.

3. While standing up, take a deep breath and then hold it as you tighten

your whole body. Start with your toes, feeling them curl and tense, then feeling that tightness move all the way up your legs, into your torso and then up into your head and down your arms. Make fists with your hands and scrunch up your face as you tighten every muscle. Hold your breath and this tightness for as long as you possibly can. Exhale with a big sigh, releasing the tension from your body as you imagine all that pent-up anger flowing out of your feet and into Earth to be alchemised. Repeat this practice three to five times, or until you feel a sense of calm even when tightening your body and holding your breath.

Repeat this practice as often as you like, or whenever you're feeling infuriated.

REFLECTIONS

- *Where in your body do you feel anger and rage most intensely?*
- *What happened to your body once you released anger?*

RELEASE RAGE IN HEALTHY WAYS, USING AWARENESS OF THE BODY AND HELP FROM MOTHER EARTH.

Let Go
of Fear

Let's be real: facing the realities of climate change's impact on the planet is frightening. It can make us want to run away by avoiding the topic altogether. It can also make us stay so busy in our lives that we don't ever have to deal with how we really feel about it all.

The thing is, that fear lives in our body, even when we try to avoid it. So instead of running away from these feelings, let's move them through our bodies.

1 Standing next to a big, strong, sturdy tree and take a moment to ground yourself by standing tall and imagining roots growing from your feet down into Earth. Inhale deeply, imagining these roots pulling supportive energy from Earth up into your body. Placing both palms against the tree, take a step back with one foot so that you are lightly pushing against the tree. Inhale deeply, and as you exhale, push against the tree as hard as you can. Vocalise any noise that wants to emerge from within you as you keep pushing. Switch legs and repeat. When you have finished, place one hand on your heart and one hand on the tree in gratitude.

2 Standing with your feet hip distance apart, ground your energy (as above). Begin by taking a deep breath and then start marching on the spot. Increase your speed until you are running as fast as you can for as long as you can. Breathe deeply and then repeat once or twice more.

3 Shaking and bouncing your body is another excellent way to release stored fear. In this practice, you'll shake your body in any way that feels good to you. Start by shaking your arms into your shoulders and chest, then move down your torso to your waist, hips and legs. Finally, move that shake all the way back up your body to your neck and head. Keep doing this until you feel a sense of release within you. For more of Nature's support, shake one of your large houseplants (if you have one) at the same time to mimic winds and help the plant grow stronger.

....

REFLECTIONS

- *Where in your body do you feel anxiety and fear most intensely?*
- *What happened to your body once you let go of fear?*
- *How can you incorporate healthy fear release into your daily habits?*

Take Your Power Back

Fawning – the tendency to want to please and serve others by placing their needs before our own – often leaves us feeling empty, disempowered and numb. Fawning keeps us from holding those most responsible for Earth's damage accountable and makes us believe that the climate crisis is too complex for us to fix. Guilt and shame for not taking enough personal action to promote sustainability increase when we're fawning, as does a stronger sense of powerlessness over the current treatment of Earth.

Let's take some of our personal power back through somatic practices that help us move through the fawn response.

1. Standing next to a large tree or plant (or near a window with a view of trees), ground yourself by imagining roots from your feet entering Earth. Breathe deeply as you feel your roots receive Earth's grounded support, pulling it up into your body with every inhale. Keep some distance between you and the plant(s) as you place your hands together in front of your heart and gently squat. Take a deep breath in and out, and on your next inhale, straighten your legs as you move your hands in an upwards swan-dive motion. As you exhale, release your hands, letting them circle back down and around you, as you come back down into a gentle squat. Each time you inhale and stretch upward, imagine yourself growing taller like the trees around you, and each time you exhale, imagine a bubble of light expanding around you. Repeat until you feel energised and strong.

2 Sitting or standing, indoors or out, think of an animal with claws and a mighty roar that you want to connect with, such as a bear, lion, tiger, leopard, jaguar or panther. Taking a deep breath into the lower stomach, make claw shapes with both hands, bringing them back to your shoulders as you arch your back. While exhaling, slowly push your clawed hands away from you, stretching your back as you howl or growl the word 'No'. Feel yourself strong in your NO as you imagine yourself pushing away all those who say a sustainable future isn't possible, or who hinder our progress towards that future.

3 Find a spot where you feel safe and secure, indoors or out. Put on one of your favourite songs to dance to, and then just let loose. Dance your heart out without judging your dance or moving for anyone else's gaze. Let the music flow with your body as you move in any way that feels right for you in this moment. When you're done, place your hands over your heart, feeling the beat of your own rhythm. Breathe deeply and take note of what you're feeling in your body.

∙∙

REFLECTIONS

- *How do you feel in your body after attempting these practices?*
- *How can you incorporate this somatic work into your self-care routine?*

Take
Up Space

The freeze response is when our nervous system responds to fear and overwhelm with a type of temporary paralysis, like a deer caught in headlights. If we tend towards freezing when stressed, we may often find ourselves procrastinating, mindlessly scrolling on our phones, diminishing our own capabilities, isolating ourselves or making ourselves small – all the while feeling overwhelmed and even depressed. Thankfully, we can use somatic practices to move through the freeze response and come back to more emotional well-being and empowerment.

1 Standing outdoors, or anywhere with a view of trees, feel your feet firmly planted on the ground. Root into your stance and feel yourself supported by Earth. Gently sway and rock your body in any way that feels good. Then place your hands just in front your ribcage, palms facing toward you. Take a deep inhale, and as you exhale, begin to twist firmly and rapidly from the ribcage area, inhaling and exhaling deeply and repeating for as long as feels good for you. Roll your hips a few times in both directions. Then come back to rocking and swaying like a tree in the wind, and this time, wrap your arms around yourself in a big hug as you continue to sway and twist.

2 Standing outdoors or in, plant your feet and feel them root into Earth. Breathe deeply as you imagine receiving from Earth with every inhale and giving back to her with every exhale. Inhaling deeply, sweep your arms up over your head as you come up on your toes. As you exhale deeply, fall back on your heels and let your arms sweep downward, hitting the sides of your thighs on the way down. Repeat until you feel more energised and alert.

3 Put on one of your favourite sad songs (you know, the one you play when you want a good cry). Dance and move your body slowly to the song, letting yourself move with any emotions that are coming up, especially grief. Dance or move with the feelings of these emotions instead of processing, analysing and overthinking them. Please note, grief is love. It's proof of our love and care for this world and each other. As we live through these times, grief is imperative for keeping our hearts open. Letting ourselves grieve for all that's been lost, and all we're still losing, is imperative. Grief is love and Earth needs our love. We need our love.

··

REFLECTION

- *How does the freeze response show up in your life?*

Forest Bathing Mindsight: A Walking Meditation

Forest bathing, or spending time immersed with the trees and their forest communities, has been proven to positively influence our health through both our nervous and immune systems. Healing forest excursions don't only occur in remote places; they can also take place in urban, suburban and rural wooded parks. The healing powers of trees and plants comes from being truly present with them. Forest bathing is less about an action and more about a state of being. It's about full immersion in the Nature around you, bearing witness to the intelligence, interconnectivity and beauty of life.

1. Start by identifying one or two wooded trail(s) or park(s) near your home. Make a plan to walk a trail at least twice during the week.

2. Before setting out, set the intention to be aware and present during this walking meditation. (Note: Please also be sure to follow safety practices so that you feel secure throughout your walk. If you don't feel safe walking alone, you can always invite someone to share this moving meditation with you.)

3. As you begin your walk, take note of the trees and plants you see surrounding you. Instead of trying to identify and label them, notice their shape, the colours, and the feeling you get inside when you fully look at them, appreciating their presence.

4. As you continue walking, allow your thoughts to flow through your mind like clouds moving across the sky. As a thought arises, acknowledge its presence and then see it simply floating away.

5. Keep walking, noticing and sensing the environment you're in. Hone in on your senses by focusing on five things you can see, four things you can smell, three things you can hear and two things you can touch.

6. Deepen your breath as you continue to move through Nature. Notice when you're holding your breath or breathing shallowly, and when you deepen and elongate your inhales and exhales.

7. Walk at any pace that feels right for you, allowing the rhythmic movement of both sides of your body to soothe your mind as you stay open and present to the world around you. As you move, fully observe, listen to and feel the organisms around you.

8. Appreciate the beauty of the space you're in. Instead of looking for evidence of damage, take note of the sunlight dancing on the leaves of the plants and the noises of birds, buzzing insects and rustling leaves. See how Nature keeps persisting, trusting that you can, too.

Once you've mastered this moving meditation in wooded areas, you can bring this level of awareness and presence to any walks you are taking, whether those be in urban, suburban or rural environments. This practice helps you focus on the beauty and positivity of Nature that still surrounds us despite the environmental challenges we face.

Forest Bathing is Medicine

Popularised by the Japanese, forest exposure therapy, also known as forest bathing, or *shinrin-yoku*, promotes the use of forests for stress reduction and immune system support. Dr Qing Li, one of the foremost experts on forest bathing, discovered that two hours spent breathing in plant chemicals in the forest reduces inflammation, blood pressure, heart rate and stress hormones, while increasing the body's production of special cancer-killing white blood cells, called natural killer cells.

The more time we spend in the forests breathing in the scents of the plants (also called phytoncides), the more our body produces these specialised protective cells.

Forest bathing can also help us move from the sympathetic nervous system's stress response into the parasympathetic nervous system's relaxation response. Physically and mentally, time spent with trees benefits our health and well-being.

Plant Scents for Self-Care

From the wafting perfume of a rose, to the resiny scents of trees, herbal smells of sage brush, and even the smell of freshly cut grass, plant scents are so much more than just aromas. They are language in chemical form – it's how plants communicate with one another. They release these special chemical scents for many reasons, including attracting beneficial organisms and warning other plants of incoming threats from pests, disease or human disturbance. The aromatic language of plants also communicates with us, positively influencing our health.

Aromatherapy is the practice of using the chemical scents of plants for therapeutic reasons, mainly through essential oils. Our sense of smell connects with the same part of our brain that creates emotional memories and responses, meaning smells can positively influence our mental health and stress levels. By intentionally inhaling certain plant scents, we invite in more emotional well-being.

1 Begin the week by bringing your attention to the natural smells that already surround you. Whenever you find yourself outdoors, slow down, giving yourself the time and space to smell the trees, flowers, herbs and plants around you. Orient yourself to the pleasant scents of Nature. Smell the blooming flowers or the bark of a tree and then a leaf or needle if it's a coniferous tree. Tip: If the leaf or needle has no smell at first, gently fold it to release some of the phytoncides within, and then smell the crease you created.

2 As the week progresses, bring your attention to the smells of plants within your home and workspaces. Before eating fruits and vegetables, take a few seconds to really smell them, noting your body's response to their aromas.

3 Intentionally use plant aromas for different purposes. For example, smell roses before interacting with a loved one, smell mint before engaging in public speaking, and sniff on a rosemary sprig when learning something you want to remember.

4 Purposely bring natural smells you enjoy into your home with flowers, naturally fragranced candles, small potted herbs and by diffusing essential oils like spruce, juniper, cypress, tea tree, eucalyptus, sandalwood, cedarwood, pine, lavender, lemon and hinoki (a type of cypress).

···

REFLECTIONS

* Which natural scents do you really enjoy?
* How can you continue to use Nature's aromas for your benefit?

A Note on Essential Oils

Essential oils are plant chemicals in highly concentrated forms, made by extracting powerful phytoncides from the leaves, seeds, stems, flowers, roots, bark and peel of plants. When diffused, essential oils cleanse the air while positively influencing our emotions.

When working with essential oils, it's important to note that a little goes a long way and not all oils are safe for everyone, especially those under ten, pregnant women and people with epilepsy or lung issues. As such, please do your research before using essential oils.

Connect with
Your Mother Tree(s)

The scientific belief used to be that trees and plants in forests were in competition with one another, each one striving to gain access to the best sunlight and soil resources. Yet thanks to the research of Canadian forest ecologist and professor, Suzanne Simard, it became clear that forests, and the many trees and plants within them, are actually collaborative communities connected through underground networks of roots, fungi and microbes known as the mycorrhizal, or mycelium, network (more on that in the next self-care practice).

At the heart of these forest communities are the 'Mother Trees', the older trees connecting with and nourishing the younger trees and plants around them. These Mother Trees nurture many forest plants, sending water, nutrients like carbon and nitrogen, and messages through their interconnected root systems. Mother Trees are even able to recognise their own progeny, and sometimes choose to send them extra nourishment.

Let's intentionally connect with the wisdom and nourishment of our own Mother Trees, those special trees that just grab our attention and awareness, whether they are near our homes or workplaces, or along our commutes or favourite trails.

Set the intention to take a few minutes each day to acknowledge and breathe with these trees. You can physically stand or sit with them if they're on your property or in public areas. You can also just be near the trees and connect with them by looking at them. On those days when you cannot see your Mother Trees, try connecting with them through your imagination.

1. Standing or sitting, place one hand on your lower abdomen and one over your heart as you breathe in deeply. On your exhale, imagine roots spreading from your feet down into Earth. See or feel your roots connecting with the roots of your Mother Tree(s).

2. Breathe deeply, imagining your whole body pulling in nourishment from the Mother Trees and Earth as you inhale, and releasing stress from your mind and body with every exhale. You can choose to connect with each tree on its own, or with your whole group of Mother Trees as one.

3. Breathe this way for a few minutes, releasing thoughts as they arise while taking note of any physical sensations within your body as you breathe with your Mother Tree(s).

4. Ask your Mother Tree(s) for the nourishing guidance they have for you. Be still, breathe and listen.

....

REFLECTIONS

- *Take note of any physical sensations experienced during this practice.*
- *What guidance did the Mother Trees have for you?*

CONNECT WITH THE WISDOM AND NOURISHMENT OF SPECIAL TREES THAT GRAB YOUR ATTENTION AND AWARENESS.

Rooting In

Living among and all around the roots of trees and plants are millions of collaborative and diverse microscopic fungi and bacteria, called the mycorrhizal (or mycelium) network. This interconnected community provides the plants with extra water and nutrients like nitrogen and carbon, while also sending chemical signals (or communications) from the roots of one plant to another. The fungi within the network create tiny, lace-like threads, which bore into the root systems of plants. This connects individual plants to a vast and communicative network which some scientists like to refer to as the 'Wood Wide Web'. The presence of the mycorrhizal network is a beautiful reminder of the importance of collaboration and support.

Speaking of support, grounding (also called 'earthing') refers to therapeutic practices that connect us with Earth's energy and electrical pulses. Grounding is a popular topic these days because so many feel disconnected from Nature and overwhelmed by the stressors of our modern world. According to research, grounding benefits our health by reducing inflammation and chronic pain, improving cardiovascular health and alleviating feelings of fatigue, anxiety and depression.

Let's ground into Earth and energetically connect with the mycorrhizal network to gain a greater sense of support, belonging, connection and vitality. This practice can be done indoors or out, with bare feet or shoes on.

1. Find a quiet spot where you are not likely to be disturbed, preferably close to a tree or plant.
2. Begin by sitting or lying down in a comfortable position. Then become aware of your breath, focusing on the feeling of air moving into your body

with every inhale and out of your body with every exhale. Continue with this breath awareness until you feel a sense of settling or anchoring into your body.

3 On your next exhale, imagine glowing roots extending from your feet and your sitting bones and gliding into Earth below you with grace and ease. Continue to breathe deeply and slowly as you imagine these roots spreading into the soil.

4 As you inhale, imagine the mycorrhizal network in its lacy intricacy, spreading and embracing your roots. As you exhale, feel or sense your roots begin to connect with the community of plants that surround you. Inhale, deeply breathing in the support of the Wood Wide Web. Then exhale deeply, feeling breath, support and connection to Earth settle within your body.

5 Keep breathing deeply. If you have any areas of pain, imagine Earth's energy moving specifically to those areas with every exhale.

6 Ask Earth and the root communities to provide you with guidance. Be still, breathe and listen.

7 When you feel complete, give thanks to the root communities, to Earth and to yourself for taking time for this practice. Slowly wiggle your fingers and toes, give your body a gentle shake and open your eyes.

This grounding practice is especially helpful when feeling overwhelmed, stressed, impatient, lonely, exhausted or under the weather.

....

REFLECTIONS

- *What was your emotional state prior to this practice?*
- *What is your emotional state after completing this practice?*
- *What did you notice and feel while breathing in support from Earth, the plants and the mycorrhizal network?*

Guided Tree Meditation

It's empowering to know that forests, plants and their interwoven communities impact our health in positive and beneficial ways. It's empowering for those moments when we are fully immersed in natural spaces and is also empowering for our daily self-care practices.

One of my favourite ways to start my day is to engage in this five-minute tree meditation. This mindfulness practice never fails to help me feel both supported by Earth and energised by the Sun. This practice can be done anywhere but will feel more concentrated if done outdoors with trees.

1. Begin by finding a quiet place to stand, where you won't be disturbed for at least five minutes.
2. Gently shake or sway your body in any way that feels good as you deepen and lengthen your breath.
3. On your next exhale, imagine roots extending from your feet down deep into the Earth, until they find a place to anchor.
4. As you inhale, imagine your roots sucking up Earth's nourishment. As you exhale, feel that nourishing energy move into your body.
5. Breathe three times like this, focusing on connecting with Earth through the roots.
6. Next, bring your attention to the top of your head, imagining that a ray of sunshine is shining directly into your crown.
7. Inhale deeply, then exhale, imagining beautiful branches and leaves emerging from your head.
8. Breathe solar energy into your head with every inhale, and let that energy move into your body with every exhale.

9 Breathe like this a few times.

10 With your next inhale, feel yourself receiving energy from both the Earth and the Sun at the same time. Exhale, feeling that energy go anywhere your body most needs it. Breathe like this for as long as you like.

11 When you feel complete, send gratitude to the Earth below your feet and the Sun above. Thank yourself for taking the time to care for yourself in this way.

12 Gently wiggle your fingers and toes and sway your body from side to side. When you feel ready, open your eyes.

··

REFLECTION

• *What do you feel happening inside when you take part in this practice?*

Nature Journals:
Connect with Your Inner Landscape

Curiosity is great for our mental health. Psychologists and neuroscientists across the world have shown how curiosity is vital for healthy development and learning, along with exploration and progress. Research has even found that intentionally practising curiosity positively influences our psychological health by increasing resiliency, rates of happiness and sense of purpose, while lowering rates of negativity and depression.

Nature journals are an expressive and creative tool for cultivating curiosity as well as connecting with, appreciating, understanding and accepting the world around us. Nature journals are also a means of connecting more deeply with yourself through your curious relationship with Earth and your own perceptions.

WHAT YOU NEED
A journal (preferably with unlined paper
so that you can sketch, doodle and draw as you please)
5–10 minutes each morning and evening
for self-reflection through journalling

MORNING JOURNAL REFLECTIONS

1 Begin each entry by noting the date and season in order to ground yourself into the present moment.

2 Then take a few moments to get curious and check in with your physical, mental and emotional states by answering the following questions without judgement, shame or needing to fix anything:

- *How is your body feeling physically this morning? Do you have any areas of pain or constriction in your body? If so, where? Do you have any areas of pleasure and expansion in your body? If so, where?*
- *How are you feeling mentally this morning? Are your thoughts rushed, strained and stressed, or patient and spacious?*
- *How are you feeling emotionally this morning? What is the first and strongest emotion you feel inside? Are there more subtle emotions beneath the strong one?*

3 Finish your journalling session by writing down three things you are grateful for.

NIGHT-TIME JOURNAL REFLECTIONS

1 Share your highlight or win of the day.

2 Take note of any key observations, epiphanies or new information you received today.

3 Write down one thing you love and appreciate about being you.

Nature Journals: Connect with Your Curiosity

This week, let's use our Nature journals to get present, make observations, ask way more questions and feel connected to ourselves and the world.

WHAT YOU NEED

Your nature journal

A spot with a view of Nature, outdoors or inside

1 Open to a fresh page in your journal and note the date, your location and the weather conditions.

2 Sitting or standing, begin to observe the scene around you. Using the journal prompt 'I observe...' write down any plants, animals, items, light, textures or patterns that are catching your attention. If you're feeling artistic you can also choose to sketch what you see.

3 Using the journal prompt 'I wonder...', write down any questions you have about your observations. For example: I wonder why this plant's leaves are heart-shaped, while this one's are oval-shaped? I wonder how ants communicate with each other? I wonder if birds understand other types of birds' songs? I wonder if bees prefer to feed from flowers in the morning or evening?

Remember your explorations are not about finding answers; you are asking these questions because they harness your curiosity, so keep them coming without thinking about the answers.

4 When you have finished with your observations, begin to make some connections with your personal life by answering the following questions: Do your observations and/or questions remind you of any personal situations you may be going through? How can you use this nature-based practice as a mirror and guide for your life?

You can choose to conduct this observation and inquiry practice in the same location, or you can mix it up, finding different natural spots to conduct your Nature journalling throughout the week.

USE YOUR NATURE JOURNAL TO GET PRESENT. WRITE DOWN ANY PLANTS, ANIMALS, ITEMS, LIGHT, TEXTURES OR PATTERNS THAT CATCH YOUR ATTENTION.

Nature Journals: Shift Your Perspective

Shifting our perspective does wonders for our mental health. Too often, our minds amplify the negativity in our lives and the world, while diminishing the positivity around and within us. But we can train our minds to look for the positive through practices that help us shift our perspectives. We can learn to zoom in, finding little moments that bring us joy and pleasure, and zoom out, taking a higher view of our challenges to identify their lessons and treasures. Nature journalling helps us cultivate these new perspectives through our observation of the natural world.

WHAT YOU NEED

A plant, indoors or outdoors
Your nature journal
A comfortable space to sit and journal

1 On a blank page in your Nature journal, note the date, location and season to ground yourself into this moment. Then fold your page into three sections.

2 Choose a part of the plant you'd like to focus on. In the middle section of the page, sketch that part of the plant with as much accuracy as you can. Anything that you cannot draw, you can just label or describe with words (for example, smooth lines on the underside of the leaf). Leave room to take note of what you are observing and questioning.

3 Then identify a smaller portion of the plant for closer observation. Take time to really look at this small section of the plant, remaining open and curious as you look with intention to see. Sketch or note what you see in a different section of the paper.

4 In the last section of the page, zoom out, taking in the whole plant and sketching and/or describing it.

5 When complete, take a moment to review all you just witnessed. Which observations sparked your curiosity? How did the zoomed-in observation shift your view of the plant? What about the zoomed-out observation?

6 Consider how we can look at environmental challenges with more zoomed-in and zoomed-out perspectives. For example, a zoomed-in perspective encourages positive changes in how we personally treat the planet, encouraging local environmental engagement. Zooming in also helps us see the beauty, interconnectivity and function of the world around us right here and now. A zoomed-out perspective recognises that the systemic changes needed to stop environmental destruction must also come from governments and industries across the globe. Zooming out also helps us see how the solutions to heal Earth are also the solutions to heal society by replacing oppressive, extractive and competitive systems with those that are more inclusive, regenerative and collaborative.

Continue this practice throughout the week, shifting your observations to different plants, animals or even little habitats around you.

....

REFLECTIONS

- *What areas in your life currently need a zoomed-in perspective? Where in your life can you look more closely at the beauty of the world and when can you savour daily moments that bring you joy?*

- *Where in your life would you benefit from a zoomed-out perspective? How can you take a bird's-eye view of your own challenges and the wisdom they hold?*

Look to the Birds

Birdsong makes us feel good and the science now backs this up. Research has found that seeing or hearing birds promotes a sense of mental well-being within us that can last for hours.

The sights and sounds of flying, chirping and singing birds calms our nerves, reduces feelings of stress, and restores our focus and attention. Now that we know this, let's connect with birds around us to inspire presence, appreciation and well-being.

1 Start by bringing your awareness to the birds that exist around your home, workspace and community. Take moments throughout your day to connect with the presence of the birds. What do you see? What do you hear? Do you notice a difference in birds and their sounds during different times of day?

2 Check in with your body and mental state throughout this practice:

- *How does your body feel before you connect with the birds? What about your mind?*
- *How does your body feel during the practice? How do the birds make you feel when you watch them fly, perch and hop? What do you feel, and where in your body do you feel it, when you hear them sing? What do you notice happening in your mind and with your thoughts?*

Birds calm our nerves, reduce feelings of stress, and restore our focus and attention.

Connect with the Sounds of Nature

Sounds are powerful waves of energetic vibration that create ripples of energy within us. Consider what happens inside you when you hear a sound you enjoy, like birds singing or music you love. Now consider what happens within you when you hear sounds you dislike, such as teeth scraping against a metal fork, incessant car horns or people screaming at each other.

Sound baths are immersions into vibrations of sound that promote a sense of openness and well-being within us. We can learn to immerse ourselves in the healing sound frequencies of Nature.

1 Begin by allowing for silence and then become aware of the sounds that permeate your life.

- *What are the most frequent sounds you hear in and around your home?*
- *Which of these sounds are generated by humans, like the hum of electricity, roar of vehicles, chattering of people, snippets of music or tinkling wind chimes?*
- *Which sounds originate from the natural environment, like wind blowing through leaves, dogs barking, birds chirping or water dripping?*
- *Can you identify any sounds around your home (or workspace) that create a feeling of pleasure and/or calmness within you? Is it possible to focus more of your awareness on these calming sounds?*

2 As you get better at focusing on the sounds that bring you peace and pleasure, become more intentional when connecting with Nature's sounds throughout your day. Do you love the sound of rainstorms, yet it hasn't rained in weeks? Search for rain sounds on the internet and play them while you go about your daily routine. You can do the same for other sounds you enjoy, like ocean waves, birdsong, rainforest noises, and many more.

....

REFLECTION

- *How can you use your intentional focus on sounds to benefit your self-care routine?*

WE CAN LEARN TO IMMERSE OURSELVES IN THE HEALING SOUND FREQUENCIES OF NATURE.

Cold Water Connection

All the water that exists on Earth is all the water that has ever existed here, cycling between the oceans, skies, land and ice. Water is both an infinite and finite resource, as over 90 per cent of Earth's water exists in the oceans. However, too often we take water for granted, especially those of us privileged enough to live where water flows, hot or cold, from our taps. Yet when we really consider how precious a resource water is, we can become much more intentional with our water use.

One way to be intentional with our water usage is through cold water exposure. Recent research points to numerous health benefits, including reducing inflammation, improving circulation, strengthening the immune system and improving our mental health.

....

Here are some ways to work with cold water throughout your week:

- Begin to alternate between hot and cold water in your showers. Shower with warm or hot water for three minutes, and then cold water for one minute (or as long as you can stand). This exposure to hot and cold water acts like a pump, creating drainage within the lymphatic system as the hot water opens up our blood vessels and the cold water constricts them. End your shower with cold water.

- Use only cold water when washing your face each morning and night.

- Take a bowl as large as your face and fill it with cold water and ice cubes. Stick your head into the bowl for as long as you can, gradually increasing your time of exposure.

- Rub an ice cube over your face, and/or hold an ice cube in your hand, for as long as possible.

- Immerse yourself in a cold-water plunge tank or cold body of water, like the ocean, a pond, lake or river. (If plunging into cold bodies of water, do be sure to have a partner there with you for safety reasons.)

....

REFLECTIONS

- *How were you feeling before your cold water connection?*
- *What about afterwards?*
- *What are your favourite ways to work with cold water?*

COLD WATER CAN REDUCE INFLAMMATION, IMPROVE CIRCULATION, STRENGTHEN THE IMMUNE SYSTEM AND IMPROVE OUR MENTAL HEALTH.

Cloud Gazing

Our connection to Nature and water isn't limited to the ground, but extends up to the skies through an appreciation of clouds. Clouds are water travelling through the sky, and that thought alone blows my mind. Losing oneself in the movement, shapes, colours and textures of the clouds, through cloud gazing, is another powerful way to calm the sympathetic nervous system, reduce stress and bring more presence and creativity into our daily lives.

This week, let's care for ourselves by connecting with the clouds. This practice is not about identifying or understanding the types of clouds you're observing (unless that brings you joy, of course). Instead, this practice is about presence and wonder.

- Spend around five minutes each morning staring up at the sky and marvelling at the clouds. Take deep inhales and exhales as you watch the sky.

- Bring your Nature journal along and begin to sketch the shapes of the clouds that you see. What do you notice about the clouds? What do you wonder? What do they remind you of?

- Take breaks throughout your day to meander past a window or go outside to connect with the clouds and your own presence.

- If it's a cloudy day with no discernable clouds, take note of how that impacts your mood and energy levels. If it's a bright sunny day with no clouds in the sky, take note of how that impacts you as well.

REFLECTIONS

- *What's happening in your mind after spending time gazing at the clouds?*
- *Imagine the clouds watching you from above. How might the clouds view the world we live upon? How might the clouds view you?*

Cloud gazing is a powerful way to calm the sympathetic nervous system and reduce stress.

Connect With
Indigenous Roots

For most of history, humans have lived in connection with Nature, as opposed to the destruction we currently see. It's imperative that we remember this so that we can believe in, and create, a future that is gentler on Earth and all who live upon her. Thankfully, there are still indigenous people across the globe who hold the answers we currently seek when it comes to healing our relationship with Earth and each other.

Indigenous communities have maintained ancient wisdoms about ecosystem functions, medicinal and edible plants, and living lightly on the land, despite centuries of abuse, forced assimilation and attempted annihilation. Indigenous people are also at the forefront of protecting Nature, from the defense of clean water to fossil fuel resistance and the protection of old growth forests. By acknowledging and learning from the land-based practices of indigenous peoples across the globe, recognising the history of the land we currently live upon and honouring our own land-based ancestry, we strengthen our roots as co-tenders of Earth.

- Spend some time researching the history of the land you currently live on. Who lived there 100 years ago? What about 1,000 years ago? How did they survive off the land and how did they work with Nature? Can the plants and animals they relied on still be found around you now?

  For example, I currently live northeast of San Diego, California, on land that for many thousands of years was occupied by both the Kumeyaay and Luiseño (Payómkawichum) peoples. They actively maintained the ecosystems in which they lived, so they would thrive, using agricultural practices (like selective harvesting) and the periodic controlled burning of forests. I still see many of the same species of plants and animals that they did on my walks and hikes, like prickly pear cactus (*Opuntia*), lemonade berry (*Rhus integrifolia*), coyotes, quails, lizards and hawks.

- Look into your own ancestry to see if you can trace your family's geographical origins and the types of land-based practices that existed there.

- Listen to and amplify the voices of indigenous wisdom keepers and support their protection of the planet. For example, Aniwa and Amazon Watch.

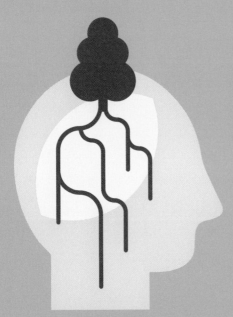

INDIGENOUS PEOPLE ACROSS THE GLOBE HOLD THE ANSWERS WE SEEK WHEN IT COMES TO HEALING OUR RELATIONSHIP WITH EARTH.

> **'Art is harmony parallel with nature.'**
>
> **— Paul Cézanne**

Creating with Nature strengthens our relationship with Earth and with ourselves.

When we intentionally use Nature as our muse, we connect with the co-creative relationship we are meant to have with Earth. From interior design and gardening to crafting art and body care products, there are infinite opportunities for us to co-create more well-being and inspiration in our lives using Nature's influence. The following self-care practices will help you engage artistically with Nature while awakening your inner creative.

CREATE
WITH
NATURE

Biophilia Hypothesis

There's a reason plants and animals inspire us and make us feel better. That reason is biophilia. First defined by psychologist Erich Fromm in the 1970s, biophilia refers to humans' 'passionate love for life and all that is alive'. The Harvard entomologist E.O. Wilson popularised this term with his biophilia hypothesis, which states that humans are biologically inclined to be drawn to and love other species, because we evolved living alongside Nature. According to biophilia, our love for life is literally written into our DNA.

It makes sense then that human cells function better with exposure to Nature. Biophilia is the knowledge that living in connection and creation with Nature benefits our health and happiness.

Biophilic Design

While biophilia speaks to our love for and connection with other living things, biophilic design is how we bring nature into our built places to create spaces that look and feel more attractive, inspiring and restorative. On a collective level we can use biophilic design to create homes, buildings, businesses and even communities that are more inviting and sustainable, with energy-efficient and waste-reducing features, as well as lots of Nature-based materials and designs. On a personal level, we can utilise biophilic design to create inspiring and restorative spaces filled with natural elements.

Uncover Your Relationship with Nature

Before you begin bringing Nature into your spaces, take some time to identify your current relationship with biophilic design by observing and recognising how Nature currently influences the look and feel of your spaces. Take note of where you're connecting with Nature in your interior spaces either through your décor or view.

- Conduct a biophilic design audit for your home and/or workspace: Where are you already decorating with items inspired by Nature or with natural materials? Where might you benefit from adding more natural décor, like plants, crystals or paintings of natural settings?
- Notice your windows and exposure to the outdoors. Which windows provide you with your favourite views, and which ones look out at your least favourite views? Are you currently utilising your favourite windows for their views? If not, can you?
- Do you have outdoor areas where you can sit with Nature? If so, are these areas inviting and comfortable for you?
- Take note of the way that sunlight moves through your home and workspace during the day. Which windows provide the most sun exposure and at what times? Are you currently taking advantage of this natural light?
- Lean into appreciating and using the Nature in your home. Bask in the Sun's rays through your windows, sit with your plants or simply take notice of your views.

Styling with Houseplants

Bringing plants indoors is one of the easiest and most accessible ways to design and decorate with Nature. The plants don't just make our spaces look better, they also help make us and our spaces feel better, too. Numerous studies have pointed to the positive impacts a view of plants has on our mental health, such as reducing stress, helping us to feel more creative, focused and productive, boosting self-esteem, increasing positivity and highlighting satisfaction. Additionally, indoor plants freshen our air by producing fresh oxygen, while purifying the air of some contaminants.

1 Determine the right plants for you by getting clear on your space, your lifestyle and the plants that are a good match for you.

- Know your space: Understand the light in your home to ascertain the best places to put your plants. Where do you get the most sunlight? Also be aware of air flow. Where do you have natural air flow and where does the air stagnate? Avoid placing plants on or next to radiators or directly under the vents for central air systems and heat.
- Know your lifestyle: Be realistic about the amount of care you're currently able to give your plants, as some need much more attention than others. Also connect with your inner stylist to determine how and where to display your plants. Do you prefer colourful pottery, neutral terracotta or woven baskets?
- Know your plants: Some houseplants are independent and resilient, while others are finicky and needy. Some prefer shaded sunlight, while others prefer direct sun. Research the plants you want to ensure they align with your space and lifestyle.

PLANTS THAT PREFER:	LOW (SHADED) SUNLIGHT	MEDIUM (INDIRECT) SUNLIGHT	BRIGHT (DIRECT) SUNLIGHT
LOW WATER & HUMIDITY	Snake plant (Sansevieria) String of pearls (Curio rowleyanus) Golden pothos (Epiprenum aureum) ZZ plant (Zamioculcas zamiifolia)	Jade plant (Crassula ovata) Houseleek (Sempervivum) Aloe vera Hoya Dracaena	Echeveria Succulents Aloe vera Cacti Dracaena Geranium
MEDIUM WATER & HUMIDITY	Various Philodendron Swiss cheese plant (Monstera deliciosa)	Alocasia Begonia Bromeliads Spider plant (Chlorophytum comosum) Fiddle leaf fig (Ficus lyrata) Rubber tree (Ficus elastica) Philodendron Syngonium Chinese evergreen (Aglaonema acutispathum) Diffenbachia Orchids	Palms Croton (Codiaeum variegatum) Ivy (Hedera)
HIGH WATER & HUMIDITY	Ferns	Ferns Peace lily (Spathiphyllum wallisii) Caladium Calathea Prayer plant (Maranta leuconeura) Peperomia	Bird of paradise (Strelitzia reginae) Zebra plant (Goeppertia zebrina)

2 Build your collection one plant at a time, ease your way into caring for your plants and take note of how they care for you and your space in return.

. . . .

REFLECTION

• *How do plants impact the feel of your space(s)?*

21

Decorate with the Elements

Biophilic design can also be expressed by decorating with the four main elements of Water, Earth, Fire and Air. While each of these elements represents what they are, they also symbolise a physical aspect of the human form: Earth is our bones, Water our blood, Fire our heartbeat and Air our breath. The elements also reflect certain traits and energies. Water is our emotions and intuition, Earth is our physical health and safety, Fire is our motivation and passion, and Air is our mindset and focus. Water guides while Fire invigorates; Earth supports while Air communicates.

We can invite the energy of the elements into our spaces with intentionally placed décor items.

1 Begin by reviewing the chart below to determine the types of elemental décor you may already possess in your home.

EARTH	WATER	FIRE	AIR
Pottery, natural woods, stone, woven baskets and blankets, tiles, plants and photographs of landscapes	Water fountains, aquariums and fish bowls, flowers or plants in water, diffusers, humidifiers, seashells, mirrors, glass, images of water	Candles, incense, fireplaces, firepits, pyramid-shaped objects (resembling a bonfire), lamps, light fixtures and images of flames	Feathers, wind chimes, flags or banners, fans, plants (for the air purification they provide) and images of clouds and skyscapes
Grounding crystals like agate, black tourmaline and onyx	Water-aligned crystals like aquamarine, labradorite and pearl	Fire-aligned crystals like garnet, obsidian, fire opal and pyrite	Air-aligned crystals like aventurine, blue calcite and celestite

2 Determine where you could use more Earth, Fire, Water and Air. Do you want more growth in your career? Bring more Earth into your workspace. How about more focus and communication? Bring in Air. Want more passion in the bedroom? Bring in Fire. Need to cool things down a bit and get into your emotions? Bring in Water.

3 Have fun as you decorate with items that inspire yet ground you.

....

REFLECTION

• *What are some of your favourite ways to decorate with the elements?*

Air:

Fire:

Water:

Earth:

WATER GUIDES
WHILE FIRE INVIGORATES;
EARTH SUPPORTS
WHILE AIR COMMUNICATES.

Create Your Nature Restoration Spot

Attention Restoration Theory, proposed by environmental psychologists Stephen and Rachel Kaplan, states that views of Nature provide our over-stimulated minds with opportunities to rest, reflect and restore. This restoration then improves our ability to intentionally direct our attention, focus and creativity. According to Attention Restoration Theory, exposure to Nature allows our brains and nervous systems to reset in ways that actually support greater attention, productivity and positive feelings.

According to the Kaplans' theory, there are four essentials that make for a restorative environment:

BEING AWAY: Being separate and away from your daily worries, responsibilities and stressors.

FASCINATION: You're attentive without effort or needing to focus in any specific way.

EXTENT: The space feels easeful, comfortable, coherent and familiar.

COMPATIBILITY: You feel intrinsically motivated to be in the space due to your own personal preferences.

Once we understand these four key components, we can use them to create our own restorative spaces, inspired by Nature.

1 Begin by identifying an area within your home and/or workspace where you can create a restorative Nature-based spot. This can be as big as a room or as small as a window seat or shelf. Start by removing items that are distracting or remind you of your daily stressors, to accentuate the sense of being away.

2 Decorate your spot with Nature-inspired décor items like plants and/ or photos of Nature – for example, stones, crystals, seashells, sticks and feathers collected from your outdoor adventures. Use plants, items and images with interesting shapes, patterns and textures. Also stay open to changing up the décor from time to time to keep this space feeling fascinating for you.

3 The extent to which you are able to engage with this space is determined by comfort, so make it as cosy as possible. Use a favourite chair, pouffe or floor pillow to create an area that encourages you to sit, observe, reflect, journal, meditate and just be.

4 Be sure that the items you choose for your Nature Restoration Spot are compatible with your tastes, preferences, values and desires, as opposed to decorating according to popular trends. This is a space for your connection and restoration, not a performance space for social media. Spend time in this space when you feel truly motivated to be there, instead of pressurising yourself to do so for specific amounts of time per day or week.

....

REFLECTION

• *How does your Nature Restoration Spot make you feel?*

Nature provides our over-stimulated minds with opportunities to rest, reflect and restore.

Create a
Plant Arrangement

Creating living art with plants engages our senses and connects us with the present moment. Being fully engaged in the here and now is a wonderful antidote to eco-anxiety. In the present moment we let go of shame from the past and fear of the future and can centre ourselves with the beauty of Nature.

When it comes to choosing the right plants, consider the type of arrangement you want to create. For example, for drier and sunny areas, a succulent arrangement, either indoors or out, would be ideal. Fern and tropical plant arrangements work well in humid and shaded areas, while houseplant arrangements are wonderful for sunlit interiors.

PLANT PAIRING SUGGESTIONS

For low-light succulent arrangements, consider a mix of *Gasteria*, *Haworthia*, jade plants (*Crassula ovata*) and snake plants (*Sansevieria*).

For bright light succulent arrangements, consider using varied Echeveria, *Aeonium*, jade plants and *Graptopetalum*.

For houseplant arrangements, consider choosing plants with similar needs.

For example, pair a *Sansevieria* or ZZ plant (*Zamioculcas zamiifolia*) with pothos *(Epipremnum)* and *Philodendron* for an arrangement that prefers shaded light and less water. Pair ferns with *Alocasia*, *Calathea* and *Syngonium* for an arrangement that prefers more water and humidity.

WHAT YOU NEED

A planting vessel (preferably with a drainage hole)
Potting compost suitable for your choice of plants
Plants that complement each other
Optional: Decorative items to enhance the plant arrangement such
as preserved moss, stones, crystals, sculptural twigs or driftwood

....

1 Gather your plants, planter, potting compost and decorative pieces. For visual interest, consider choosing plants that act as thrillers, fillers and spillers. Thrillers are the main focus due to their size, shape, colour or texture. Fillers are more neutral plants that take up space, while spillers hang or twine out of the planting vessel.

2 Add potting compost to your planter and then add the plants and more potting mix, ensuring all their roots are fully buried.

3 Use plants of different heights to draw in the eye. If your arrangement has a set front and back, place the tallest plants at the back and the shortest plants up front. If your arrangement will be looked at from all angles, consider positioning the tallest plant in the centre of the vessel, then placing the shorter plants around the centrepiece.

4 Add your (optional) décor pieces in any way you like. Remember there is no right or wrong way to do this! Trust your eye and release any need for perfection.

5 Water your living art and place near a source of sunlight, indoors or out, depending on your plants' needs.

....

REFLECTIONS

* *How was your mood and mindset prior to engaging in this practice?*
* *How about afterwards?*

Botanical Art

Practising art is an act of self-care. When we use natural subjects as the inspiration for art, we also connect deeply with the beauty and function of Nature. We connect with the awe and love we feel for Earth. We connect with the joy and pleasure of appreciation despite the very real challenges we face.

WHAT YOU NEED
Your journal or some sketching paper
Something to write, paint or sketch with, such as
watercolours and brushes, coloured pencils or pens

1. Spend time each day using your preferred medium(s) to engage more closely with Nature. Find a leaf with a pattern you like and sketch, draw or paint it. Sketch or paint the trees, clouds, blooms or anything from Nature that enthralls you. Or simply spend time creating in Nature, allowing yourself to flow with the shapes and colours you put on the page.

2. Remember, this practice isn't about painting or sketching a perfect leaf or flower; it's about engaging with Nature and yourself through creativity. Let the process be the purpose.

REFLECTION

- *How do you feel prior to practising art?*
- *What do you feel when in the creative process?*
- *How do you feel after your artistic self-care session?*

**Spend time creating
in Nature, allowing
yourself to flow with
the shapes and colours
you put on the page.**

Caring for Bonsai Jade

Bonsai, which literally translates as 'tree planted into shallow container' in Japanese, is a practice of horticulture, art and presence that's been around for over a thousand years. Originally practised in ancient China and then adapted by Japanese Zen Buddhists, the art of bonsai is about growing a miniature yet realistic tree.

Creating and caring for bonsai benefits our mental health. Consistently pruning the plant promotes mindfulness, presence, focus and concentration. Spending time creating and maintaining bonsai plants also promotes self-reflection, self-awareness and pride over our botanical accomplishment. It turns out that shaping our plants also provides us opportunities to shape our thoughts and moods.

Let's create our own bonsai using a readily accessible and easy-to-maintain plant, jade (*Crassula ovata*). Jade is a great option for bonsai because you can use a simple clipping from a larger plant (as long as the roots aren't overly developed), and they have strong yet flexible stems and branches that are easy to prune and shape.

WHAT YOU NEED
A clipping of jade plant that's about 13–25 cm (5–10 in)
A shallow planting vessel, preferably with a drainage hole
Clean secateurs or scissors
Succulent potting compost or one mixed with horticultural sand
or pumice for better drainage
Optional décor items (see page 69 for suggestions)
Chopstick
Spoon

1. Before planting your jade clipping, give it a first prune and shaping. Clip away any stems or branches close to the base and remove any extra-large leaves. Clip away stems or leaves that keep the plant looking like a bush, leaving behind the ones that most resemble the branches of trees.

2. Place the free-draining potting compost in the shallow planting vessel until it is about 2.5 cm (½ in) from the top.

3. Using the spoon, dig a small hole and plant your jade clipping. Cover with more potting compost.

4. Use natural elements like stones, wood, decorative moss and crystals to decorate around the newly planted jade.

5. If the clipping you planted already has roots, water immediately after planting. If it didn't have roots, wait about two weeks before watering to give them time to grow.

6. Place your jade bonsai near a source of natural light. Continue to artfully prune back the growth of the plant to create a miniature 'tree' created by you and Nature in tandem.

• •

REFLECTIONS

- *What happens in your mind and body when you're immersed in creating and caring for your bonsai?*
- *What else could use some pruning and reshaping in your life?*

CARING FOR BONSAI BENEFITS OUR MENTAL HEALTH.

Painting with Plants

Plant-based art can also be created from plant material alone, as seen in the inspired work of artist and author Vicki Rawlins (which you can check out in her book *The Power of Flowers*). Vicki uses found plant materials like leaves, twigs, petals, roots, bark and seeds to create magnificent impermanent illustrations of life.

Let's use natural materials as the medium for our artistic expression in this temporary yet inspiring way.

WHAT YOU NEED

Black or white construction paper for the background

Tape

Numerous varieties of found plant materials like

twigs, leaves, petals, blooms, seeds and pieces of bark

Scissors

Tweezers

A camera

1 Begin by going on a Nature walk to gather materials for your plant painting. Make sure you're only collecting materials in permitted areas. Collect first from fallen leaves, flowers and petals, prior to clipping fresh materials.

2 Make some space on a tabletop indoors, preferably in an area with good natural light. Tape the edges of your construction paper down to flatten it and keep it secured.

3 Spread out your plant materials and look closely at them, letting their shapes, colours and textures inspire you. What can you imagine creating with the materials you have at hand? A face, a scene, an animal, an abstract pattern?

4 Use the scissors to cut materials as you need them and the tweezers to place and manipulate these into shapes on the construction paper. Continue to find inspiration in natural items, adding stones, seashells, feathers or crystals to your scene.

5 When your art piece feels complete, use the camera to capture your creation. Give thanks to Nature, the materials and yourself for taking part in this practice, and then deconstruct your art in any way that feels good for you. Repurpose your plant materials to be used in other forms of art, compost them or give them back to Earth.

....

REFLECTION

• *Reflect upon the impermanence of this art form. What lessons can this practice teach you about the impermanent nature of life?*

Wood Décor

In the Five Element system of feng shui (comprising Wood, Fire, Earth, Metal and Water), the element of Wood represents growth, vitality, flexibility, strength and creativity. Feng shui also states that wooden décor brings more of the supportive and expansive energies of Wood into our spaces.

Find a wooden branch, stick or driftwood piece that has a shape and/or texture that inspires you. Harvest your piece of wood responsibly by taking branches already fallen to the ground or driftwood that has washed ashore. Branches pruned from your own trees are also responsible options.

WHAT YOU NEED

A natural piece of wood that inspires you
Paint scraper
Sandpaper
Your imagination!

1. After sourcing your branch, stick or driftwood piece, use a paint scraper to remove the bark, exposing the smooth wood below.
2. Use the sandpaper to smooth down any rough spots.
3. You can use your finished wood for various things. For example, branches can be hung on walls to display seasonal décor or hang scarves and hats. You can also use large sticks and branches as houseplant supports, or simply display them as pieces of art. They also make great bases for macramé and walking sticks. Smaller pieces of driftwood can be used as shelf décor and supports for air plants.

Hammered Botanical Prints

As we learned way back in *Practice 2 Let Go of Anger*, releasing anger and rage in constructive ways is a great way to practise self-care. What if I told you there was a healthy way to release your rage that also produced a beautiful work of art? This natural craft enhances observation skills, presence and appreciation, while allowing us to bang out some heavy feelings in the process. It's also a fun one to do with kids.

WHAT YOU NEED

A variety of flowers: Choose thinner options like cosmos, pansies, wildflowers and small ground-cover flowers – the brighter the colour, the better.

Scissors or secateurs

A piece of lightweight fabric (like cotton cloth), thick cardstock or watercolour paper

Masking tape

Larger piece of cardboard (to protect your work surface while hammering)

3–4 paper or cloth napkins

....

1 Begin with a Nature walk to collect your flowers. Look for smaller and thinner flowers, and only harvest a few from each location. Wildflowers work wonderfully for this project. You can also use flowers from clipped arrangements or bouquets.

2 Arrange the flowers and leaves face down on the cloth, cardstock or paper in any arrangement that pleases you, then tape everything down with the masking tape. Tape around any thick stems that are sticking up and then clip those away. Make sure all leaves and petals are completely covered by the tape.

3 Place the piece of cardboard on your work surface to protect it, then cover with one of the paper or cloth napkins. Lay your arrangement with the taped botanicals so it is face down on the napkin, then cover with two or three more napkins.

4 Start hammering away! Let any stress and anger leave your body as you pound away.

5 Be sure to aim for the areas where the flowers are arranged. Periodically peek at your progress to ascertain how the colours are transferring.

6 Carefully pull the masking tape off and remove all plant materials from the cloth, cardstock or paper. Enjoy your new plant-themed art in a frame, as a gift card or as hand towels.

7 When complete, gift the flowers back to Nature, by composting or adding to green waste.

....

REFLECTIONS

- *What did you feel as you hammered?*
- *What do you feel when you look at the art you co-created with the generosity of Nature?*

Plan a Garden

Gardening is an act of self-care. There are many ways to engage in gardening, even if you don't have any outdoor space. Herbs, flowers and even produce can be grown in pots on bright windowsills, patios and balconies. New technologies, like hydroponic grow towers with grow lights, allow people to grow herbs and greens indoors all year round. Planting boxes that attach to walls and fences are also available, allowing those with small spaces to garden vertically. For those who don't want to garden alone, look for local community gardens where you can garden a plot of land with your neighbours. Along with the physical, mental and emotional benefits of gardening, the practice of planning a garden helps us accept the present moment as well as our positive potential, both of which translate well into our ongoing fight against climate change.

WHAT YOU NEED
Paper and pen or pencil, or notes on your phone or computer

....

1 Begin by determining the scope of your garden by answering the following questions:

- Will you be planting indoors or outdoors?
- How do you plan on watering your garden, and how often? By hand or through an irrigation system?
- What is your microclimate (the specific climate of your home and garden)? If planting indoors, assess the position, duration and strength of the sunlight in your spaces. Consider whether

you need to purchase a few indoor grow lights for your indoor plants. Also take note of air flow through the space. If planting outdoors, identify the areas of most direct and indirect sun along with your plant hardiness zone, or the minimum temperatures of a specific area so that you know which plants will thrive.

- What level of commitment can you give to this garden? For gardening to promote self-care it's important that you set yourself up for success by not overwhelming yourself with too big a project. Prepare yourself for some failure too, because life happens. In my experience, it's best to start small and grow sustainably, gathering skills and knowledge as you go.

2 Once you've identified and assessed your space, begin to research the types of plants you'd like to grow, along with the materials you'll need. Make a list of your desired planters, plants, potting compost and (optional) natural fertilisers like garden compost or worm castings. Keep in mind the season you will be planting in (some plants will not survive over winter) and when you would like your plants to flower. Possible garden options include:

- Raised bed and/or in-ground beds outside
- Raised beds, pots, growing bags or hanging planters for roof gardens, patios or decks (check weight restrictions for roof gardens)
- Window boxes for window ledges, patios or decks (always fix planters securely to ledges)
- Pots of herbs, flowers or greens near windows

3 Compare your garden list with your budget and get realistic about your goals before you start shopping. You can often find inexpensive or even free gardening materials online. Set a date and create a plan of action for getting your garden growing, no matter what its size.

••

REFLECTION

- *Where in your life can you think more positively about yourself and your potential?*

Plant a
Fruit Tree

When we plant fruit trees, we strengthen our patience and trust. Typically, it takes anywhere from two to seven years before fruit trees begin to bear fruit, with some taking even longer. When we tend to fruit trees, appreciating them as we patiently await their harvest, we also learn to do the same for ourselves. Recognising that, like the trees, our own growth is also cyclical, with seasons of growing, seasons of harvest and seasons of dormancy.

WHAT YOU NEED
A young fruit tree, about 60 cm (2 ft), for outdoor planting,
or a dwarf fruit tree for indoor planting (only tropical and subtropical trees
are suitable for growing indoors)
For outdoor planting: Garden soil and a natural fertiliser best suited to the tree
For indoor planting: A large pot with a drainage hole and water drainage
saucer, plus potting compost

....

1 Determine the type of tree you want, whether it can thrive in your environment, and where you wish to plant it – outdoors or in. Keep in mind, you'll want to give your tree six to eight hours of sunlight per day.

2 If planting outdoors, dig a hole twice as wide and deep as the root ball of your tree. Add natural fertiliser to the hole and then plant your tree. Fill in the rest of the hole with soil so that the tree appears to be growing from a mini hill of soil. Water generously.

3 If planting in a pot, be sure to use a pot twice as wide and at least as deep as the tree's root ball. Fill the pot with some potting compost, then place your plant in the pot and add more potting compost to cover the root ball. Water generousy. Keep in mind that you can also move your indoor trees outside during warmer growing months. Just be sure to keep them in shaded sunlight so they don't get burned by the sun.

4 Be sure to provide the tree with extra care, especially the first month after planting. If it feels right, name the tree and speak to it while you care for it.

INDOOR FRUIT TREES

TREE	TEMPERATURE	LIGHT	SOIL	WATER
Dwarf Meyer lemon tree *Citrus × limon* 'Meyer'	10–24°C/50–80°F	Full sun	Free-draining potting compost	Let compost dry out before watering
Dwarf key lime tree *Citrus × aurantiifolia*	18–26°C/65–75°F	Full sun	Free-draining potting compost	About once per week
Olive tree *Olea europaea*	18–29°C/65–85°F	Full sun	Free-draining potting compost	About once per week

Health Benefits of Gardening

For those who love to garden, it should come as no surprise that this practice provides lots of physical, mental and emotional benefits. On a physical level, it gets us outside, breathing fresh air and soaking up vitamin D from the sun. Gardening is also a workout, with lots of digging, bending, squatting, stretching and pulling, as anyone who has ever planted or weeded a garden can confirm. Additionally, exposure to the sights and smells of gardens influences our limbic and nervous systems in restorative ways.

On a mental health level, gardening has the potential to increase our sense of presence, capability and positive self-esteem. To plant a garden or grow any form of food is an act of trust, both in ourselves and in Nature; trusting that Earth provides all that is needed to grow food from her soils, and that we can help her do so.

Plant a Herb Garden

Herbs not only enhance the aromas and flavours of our food and drink, they also contain many plant compounds that positively impact our physical and mental health. Herbs are filled with powerful plant chemicals, many of which are antimicrobial, antiseptic and anti-inflammatory. Growing our own herbs provides us with the positive impacts of gardening along with powerful ingredients for self-care recipes like culinary creations, healing teas and tinctures, clarifying simmer pots and restorative botanical baths (more on these practices coming next!).

WHAT YOU NEED

A place to plant your herbs – pots, planters or in the ground
An area with about six hours of filtered sunlight per day
Herbs of your choice
For indoor planting: Free-draining organic potting compost
For outdoor planting: A natural fertiliser such as garden compost
or worm castings

1 Identify where you want to plant your herbs. If planting outdoors, consider the sunlight, season and temperature. If planting indoors, consider the sunlight, temperature and air flow conditions.

2 Identify the types of herbs you wish to plant. For example, for savoury cooking use plants like basil, oregano, rosemary, thyme, sage, dill,

coriander (cilantro) and parsley. For fresh teas use plants like mint, lemon balm, chamomile and borage.

3 Half-fill your planting vessel with potting compost, then arrange your herbs and add more potting compost, being sure to fully cover the root balls. If planting outdoors, dig a hole for each herb, add some garden compost or worm castings to the bottom, then plant up and backfill the holes with soil.

4 Water generously after planting. If you have planted your herbs in pots, place in an area that receives bright indirect sunlight. Water thoroughly when the top 2 cm (1 in) of potting compost is dry.

Introduction to Herbalism

Throughout human history, plants have been our medicine. In fact, much of our modern medicine was originally synthesised from natural plant chemicals. Today, many are returning to plant medicine, remembering how plants have nourished and healed us for millennia. Herbalism is the study and practice of intentionally using plants as medicinal remedies for illness and injuries. Herbalism is also about intentionally using plants to boost immunity and promote overall health and well-being. Herbalism involves using plant materials like roots, fruits, leaves, barks, petals, seeds and peels, prepared and used in teas, tinctures, salves, baths and meals. While the health benefits of herbalism are available to us all, and most herbal medicines are safe, it's important to work with a certified herbalist or naturopath if you're on medication, pregnant, nursing or dealing with specific health concerns.

Consume More Plants

Food can be either one of our greatest allies for healing and well-being, or one of our greatest foes. Likewise, how we produce and consume food can positively impact the planet, like the food forests created by the Indigenous people of the Americas prior to colonisation, or negatively impact Earth, as industrialised agriculture is doing now. When we eat more plant-based foods and attempt to source fresh produce as locally as possible, we promote health for ourselves and Earth simultaneously.

Let's practise self-care and planet care together by adding more fresh herbs and plants to our daily meals.

Here are some ways to add fresh herbs:

- In smoothies. Mint and borage are my personal favourites.
- Sprinkled in salads. Basil, thyme, mint, coriander (cilantro) and parsley are all great options.
- Sautéed in stir-fries, soups, sauces or stew. Rosemary, sage and oregano are excellent for this.
- Made into herbal teas (see *Practice 33*).

Here are some ways to add fresh fruits and vegetables:

- Chopped as snacks.
- Sautéed or puréed in sauces and soups.
- Added to sandwiches.
- Put on cereal or yogurt.
- Marinated and grilled with whatever else you're cooking.

REFLECTION

• *Do you notice any difference in the way you think and how your body feels after adding more herbs and plant-based food to your diet?*

FOOD CAN BE EITHER ONE OF OUR GREATEST ALLIES FOR HEALING AND WELL-BEING, OR ONE OF OUR GREATEST FOES.

33

Herbal Teas

One of the easiest ways to connect with the healing properties of plants is through teas. When steeped in hot water, plants release medicinal and restorative chemicals that positively impact our physical, mental and emotional health. Herbals teas are used to ease digestive issues, promote rest and sleep, soothe sore throats and enhance immunity. The act of making, serving and drinking your tea can also become a practice of deep reverence, connection and presence, as seen in tea rituals all over the world.

WHAT YOU NEED

Fresh, dried or pre-packed tea material
If using fresh leaves and flowers, you'll want about
one or two handfuls, depending on the size of your vessel
If using dried plant materials, you'll want about
1–2 tablespoons of plant material
Pot or kettle of boiling water
Cafetière (which is best for fresh herbs and flowers),
teapot or a loose-leaf tea infuser
Mug

....

1 Begin by identifying your intention for drinking the tea. Do you want to feel more energised, or more restful? Do you want to feel more communicative, or ease physical discomfort? Knowing your intention informs your tea choice. For example: Use mint and borage for a fresh, light and cooling tea; varieties of mints for easing stomach upset and enhancing communication skills; thyme and honey for soothing sore throats and coughs; and chamomile and lemon balm for promoting calmness and positivity.

2 If using plants from your own herb garden, harvest about a handful of leaves and flowers from each plant you've chosen for your tea. Appreciate the plants, Earth, your garden and yourself for this practice. If using dried herbs or pre-packaged teas, also appreciate all that brought the tea into your hands.

3 Set your water to boil, and while waiting, connect with the plants you'll be drinking. If using fresh herbs, wash and pat them dry. Cut them up to release their medicinal compounds, then place them in the bottom of your cafetière or teapot. If using dried loose-leaf tea, spoon into a tea infuser or add to a teapot. If using teabags, place a bag in your mug.

4 Let the water settle for a few moments after it boils, and then pour the hot water over your tea. Cover and let steep for at least ten minutes. Then push down the cafetiere plunger, strain away your plant material, or remove the infuser or teabag.

5 Sweeten with a little honey, if you like, and then gratefully sip your tea, preferably while enjoying a view of Nature.

....

REFLECTIONS

- *What teas are you drinking this week and why?*
- *How do you feel before your cup of tea?*
- *How do you feel during and after drinking your tea?*

Rosemary Hair Spray

Taking time to pamper your hair and scalp in ways that don't cost a lot of money or expose you to the harsh chemicals often found in haircare products is a beneficial way to care for yourself. Let's continue using Nature's ingredients to create our own self-care recipes with this scalp-clarifying and hair growth-stimulating rosemary hair spray. Rosemary's been used for centuries as a memory booster and hair growth stimulator. It also soothes itchy scalps, reduces excess hair oils, boosts hair shine and softness, and minimises dandruff, all of which makes this aromatic herb an excellent choice for hair and scalp care.

WHAT YOU NEED

8 sprigs of fresh rosemary
A pot filled with about 2 cups of water
A heat source (hob/stovetop)
A strainer
A large bowl
A funnel
Airtight glass spray bottle (sterilised)

● ●

1 Begin by adding 2 cups of water to the pot and bringing it to a boil.
2 Gratefully harvest some rosemary sprigs from your garden (or buy from a shop). Rinse them well and pat dry.

3 Leave one sprig of rosemary to the side and then roughly chop the remaining rosemary – stems and all.

4 Once the water is boiling, turn the heat to low and add your chopped rosemary, stirring to ensure all the plants are covered in water. Cover with a lid and allow to lightly simmer for about 30 minutes.

5 Turn off the heat and let the rosemary tea cool, then pour the liquid into the large bowl, using the strainer to separate out the plant material.

6 Using the funnel, pour the rosemary tea into the spray bottle. Add the whole sprig of rosemary, then seal the top of the bottle and shake well.

7 Wash and condition your hair as usual. Squeeze out any excess water from your hair and then spray the rosemary rinse all over your head, focusing especially on massaging it into your scalp.

8 While you may notice immediate improvements in your hair's shine and softness, do note that it will take weeks of using this rosemary spray to see an impact on your hair's growth.

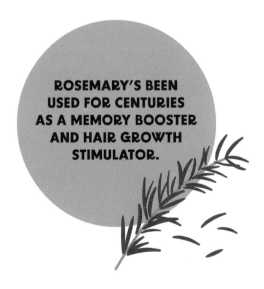

ROSEMARY'S BEEN USED FOR CENTURIES AS A MEMORY BOOSTER AND HAIR GROWTH STIMULATOR.

Botanical Baths

Baths are amazing self-care tools that can ease our physical aches along with our emotional ones. Botanical baths take this practice to the next level by infusing our bodies with the positive impacts of plant chemicals through our largest organ: our skin.

WHAT YOU NEED

Fresh or dried herbs (see the two recipes opposite for options)
A pot filled with about 3 cups of water
A heat source (hob/stovetop)
A fine-mesh strainer
A bathtub or a bowl large enough for both feet
Mixing spoon
Optional additions: Epsom salts and fresh or dried organic flowers
or petals like rose, jasmine, chamomile, chrysanthemum, yarrow,
borage, lavender and violet

....

1 Bring the water to a boil in the pot.
2 Gratefully gather and prepare the herbs and flowers by washing, drying and roughly chopping them. (Please note: If not harvesting from your own garden, please purchase organic herbs and flowers to avoid additional exposure to pesticides.) Use about a handful of each herb – stems and leaves included. For dried herbs, use 2–3 tablespoons of each.

3 Once the water is boiling, lower the heat and add your herbs to the pot. Stir well. Cover loosely and then allow to simmer gently for about 30 minutes if using fresh herbs and about 15 minutes for dried herbs.

4 While the herbs are simmering, draw your bath or prepare a foot bath.

5 Turn off the heat and pour the tea into your bathtub or foot bath, using the strainer to remove the plant materials. Stir the water round a few times.

6 If needed, add more water at the temperature of your choice.

7 Optional: Sprinkle in some fresh or dried flowers for an extra luxurious feel, not to mention a beautiful photo opportunity.

8 Check the temperature first and then slowly submerge yourself in the bathtub or plunge your feet into the foot bath, breathing deeply as you feel your body enjoy a botanically infused state of relaxation.

....

REFLECTIONS

- *How did I feel before my botanical bath?*
- *How does this experience feel different to baths I've taken before?*
- *How am I feeling afterwards?*

PHYSICAL HEALTH BATH TEA
For easing body aches and/or inflammation:

Draw a bath and add up to 2 cups of Epsom salts to the running water. In your pot, combine a handful of each fresh herb or 2 tablespoons of each dried herb:

- Rosemary
- Sage
- Chamomile
- Yarrow

MENTAL HEALTH BATH TEA
For easing negative thoughts:

Draw a bath. In your pot, combine a handful of each fresh herb or 2 tablespoons of each dried herb:

- Lemon balm
- Basil
- Chamomile
- Lavender

Botanical
Simmer Pots

Climate change and our use of fossil fuels negatively impact air quality through toxic emissions and more frequent and intense wildfires. This creates a negative impact on our respiratory health. Thankfully, Nature provides plants that can be used to naturally freshen the air while helping our lungs and respiratory systems out. One of the best ways to do this is with a Botanical Simmer pot – a pot of simmering water mixed with plants that creates a scented steam full of cleansing plant chemicals.

WHAT YOU NEED

½ lemon, sliced
1 handful of fresh or 2 tablespoons dried mint (optional)
1 handful of fresh or 2 tablespoons dried oregano
1-2 cinnamon sticks
2-3 cloves
2 tablespoons dried mullein
A pot filled with about 3–4 cups of water
A heat source (hob/stovetop)

1 Gather and prepare your materials. Pour about 3-4 cups of water into the pot and bring it to a gentle boil.

2 Add the fresh plants first (if using) and then stir in the dried herbs.

3 Reduce the heat all the way down and allow the pot to simmer for hours, as it fills your home with refreshing, health-boosting smells.

4 Spend time near the simmering pot, breathing in the steam vapours.

5 Feel grateful to the plants for providing their aromatic and chemical support! Always remember to keep an eye on the water level in the simmer pot and remove from the heat when you have finished breathing in the wonderful vapours.

'Give thanks for what you have been given. Give a gift, in reciprocity for what you have taken. Sustain the ones who sustain you and the Earth will last forever.'

— Robin Wall Kimmerer, *Braiding Sweetgrass*

We are meant to live in reciprocity with Earth.

Our breath, and even our (organic) waste, is meant to nourish and feed the plants, the soil and the planet. We are meant to tend to Earth, maintaining the balance of life, recognising our interconnectivity with the myriad species with which we share this planet.

When we take actions every day to care for the environment, we recognise that we're all part of the solutions needed to live more harmoniously on the planet. When we balance our taking with our giving, we begin to heal Earth and ourselves in the process. Especially when we take these actions from a place of connection, appreciation and love. That's exactly what we'll be doing with the following self-care practices.

GIVE
BACK TO
NATURE

When it comes to eco-anxiety,
our actions are
also our antidotes.

Practise an Attitude of Gratitude

When we acknowledge all that Earth gives to us daily, it becomes an act of reciprocal love to protect and give back to Earth in return. Let's cultivate an attitude of gratitude when it comes to Earth. Gratitude for the oxygen and inspiration from the trees and plants all around, the songs of the birds and croaks of the frogs, the textures of the clouds and colours of the flowers. Gratitude for the beauty of the rising and setting Sun, along with the air we breathe, water we drink, food we eat and all that brought that food to us. When we lean into our gratitude for Earth, it helps us remember to thank this amazing planet for all that is so generously provided to us.

WHAT YOU NEED
Your journal and pen
Exposure to Nature

....

- Each morning, before engaging with a screen, write a list of five things you're grateful for.

- Throughout the day, be conscious of truly appreciating the Nature around you, whether that be a trail or tree you love, or houseplants within your home.

- Connect with gratitude each time you eat something fresh and delicious, or when you harvest foods and herbs from your own garden.

- When you feel those moments of appreciation for Nature, consciously say thank you to Earth. You can do this by silently repeating 'Thank you' numerous times, or by sending Earth your gratitude and love on a daily basis.

....

REFLECTION

- *What do you notice about your own attitude after engaging with more gratitude for the last week?*

Breathwork with Plants

One of the clearest proofs of our reciprocal relationship with Nature is found in our breath. We rely on plants for the very oxygen we breathe. The plants in turn rely on the carbon dioxide we produce with each exhale for their own breath. Our breath feeds the plants just as their breath feeds ours.

Our breath also has a huge impact on our mental, physical and emotional health, which is why breathwork is such a beloved well-being practice. Breathwork, also referred to as Pranayama in yogic traditions, is the intentional use of inhales, exhales and breath holds to create various therapeutic states of relaxation, activation, release and euphoria within us.

This week, we'll connect more deeply with our breath, both for our own well-being and as an intentional gift to the plants and Earth.

WHAT YOU NEED

A quiet place to sit or lie down, either outdoors or in, near some plants

Your undivided attention

....

1 Once you've found your spot near plants for intentional breathing, determine whether you need more relaxation or more motivation.

- If you're feeling anxious, nervous, angry or overwhelmed, you'll want to breathe the more calming and relaxing Box Breath or Wave Breath (see page 102).
- If you're feeling sad, depressed or unmotivated, you'll want to breathe the Breath of Fire (see page 103).

2 Set a timer for anywhere between five and twenty minutes. (Note: If just beginning breathwork, start with five minutes and work your way up to longer periods of time.) Then sit down comfortably in your spot.

3 Gently close your eyes and begin to bring your attention to your breath, focusing on the sound and feel of your inhales and exhales. Focus on inhaling into the lower abdomen and releasing tension with your exhale. Breathe comfortably like this for about four breaths. Then focus on your exhale, releasing all the air from your lungs with a long, slow and deep exhale.

4 Begin to work on your intentional breaths, choosing the option on pages 102–103 that best suits your current needs. Remember to bring extra awareness to your exhales, imagining each exhale flowing directly to the plants around you.

5 Breathe in this way for as long as you like, and then allow your breath to come back to its natural pace and rhythm. Give thanks to the plants for the oxygen they create and to yourself for taking the time and effort to oxygenate yourself body, mind and soul.

INHALES, EXHALES AND BREATH CAN CREATE RELAXATION, ACTIVATION, RELEASE AND EUPHORIA WITHIN US.

Calming and Relaxing Breathwork:

Box Breath

- Inhale and exhale slowly and deeply through the nose.
- Inhale for a count of 4, and then hold your breath at the top for a count of 4.
- Then exhale for a count of 4, and hold your breath at the bottom for a count of 4.
- Repeat, drawing a box with your breath as you inhale, hold, exhale, and hold, all for 4 counts. You can also increase the count by inhaling, holding, exhaling and holding for a 6 count or an 8 count too – you decide what feels best and most calming for you.

Wave Breath

- Inhale slowly and deeply through your nose, imagining a wave being pulled back from the shore.
- Then exhale through your open mouth slowly and deeply, imagining a wave tumbling against the shore and releasing tension from your body.
- Continue inhaling the wave in and exhaling the wave out at a pace and depth that feels right for you.
- Let the rhythm of the breath calm you.

Motivating and Energising Breathwork:

Breath of Fire

- Sit up tall.
- Inhale through your nose, feeling your lower belly expand.
- Without pausing, exhale forcefully through your nose, while contracting your belly and sucking your belly button in towards your spine.
- Immediately breathe in forcefully through the nose again, filling the lower abdomen and then forcefully exhaling again through the nose. It should feel and sound as if you're panting through your nose.
- Repeat for 30 breaths. On the last breath, exhale deeply and then inhale deeply, slowing down your breath to a natural pace for about 10 seconds.
- Do another round of 30 Breaths of Fire, and then rest again.
- Finish with one last round and then breathe deeply, allowing your breath to return to its natural rhythm.

Composting 101

Healthy soils benefit plant, human and planetary health. Composting is the intentional act of turning food waste into nutrient-rich fertilisers to nourish the soil and plants without the need for chemicals. When we compost, we are part of the solution. We also witness how Nature takes our waste, lets it decay, and then transforms it into something that supports life again.

1 Determine if you have the time and space to compost. If you do, begin to look into the different methods of composting available to find the best one for you. For example:

- Composting bins that spin. Purchased or handmade, these allow for easy turning of the compost. Theywork well for smaller gardens or even large porches.
- Compost heap. The most straightforward approach of layering garden and food waste into a big pile, covering with a tarp and turning every few months. This method requires lots of outdoor space.
- Worm composting trays. These use the powerful appetite of worms to quickly break down food waste into an organic fertiliser plants love. They can be kept in the home, making them a great option for people who live in urban spaces, too.
- Modern composting machines. New technologies like the Lomi composter actually turn food waste into rich fertiliser overnight. Compact enough to fit on a kitchen worktop, these are great for urban and suburban gardeners.

2 If you don't have the time, space or desire to compost at home, look into whether your local waste management accepts food waste within their garden or green waste programme. If your waste management authority accepts garden and food waste, ask for a bin so you can start composting, too.

3 If your local waste authority doesn't compost, see if a local community or school garden accepts food waste for their composting efforts. If so, purchase a large plastic bucket with a sealing lid and use that to collect your weekly food scraps to deliver to the garden.

4 If composting is not an option for you, you can start even more simply by spreading old coffee grounds on the top of the soil of your indoor and outdoor plants. You can also support organisations that are committed to replenishing the health of the soil.

Soil Health is Planet Health

Healthy topsoil is essential for the health of the planet, yet our current methods of food production are wreaking havoc on soil vitality and fertility. Mainstream agricultural practices, such as planting acres of a single crop (for example, corn and soy), over-tilling the topsoil and spraying crops with massive amounts of synthetic pesticides, herbicides and fertilisers, are destroying the healthy functioning of Earth's soils.

Soil not only supports about 95 per cent of the food we eat, it also stores massive amounts of carbon – three times the amount found in the atmosphere – and water. Healthy soils are filled with trillions of biodiverse microbes, like those that make up the mycelium network, which benefit the growth and health of plants worldwide. These fungi may even be part of the solution to our plastic pollution problem, as researchers in Australia recently discovered two types of fungi (found in the soil) that can completely break down plastic!

Support Local Regenerative Farming

Regenerative agriculture is a system of farming that keeps the health of Earth in mind, as opposed to focusing solely on growing the most crops possible. In regenerative agriculture, farmers focus on protecting biodiversity, nourishing the soil, enriching watersheds and maintaining the healthy function of ecosystems for generations to come. Regenerative agriculture involves numerous farming practices like organic pest control and fertilisation, composting, planting cover crops during winter months, rotating crops and companion planting.

Regenerative farming doesn't just benefit Earth's health, it benefits our health as well, thanks to the production of cleaner and more nutrient-rich foods. It also allows us to eat more locally and seasonally which reconnects us to the natural cycles and rhythms of Earth, while also reducing carbon emissions.

1. Shop for produce at your local farmers' market this week, and chat with the farmers to learn more about how it was grown.

2. Join a local community supported agriculture (CSA) programme from a farm that utilises regenerative farming techniques and get a box of fresh and local produce delivered to you.

3. Search for regenerative farms around you through the Regenerative Farm Map (organicconsumers.org/regenerative-farm-map/). Support those farms if you can.

4. If you garden or grow any of your own food, companion plant herbs, nitrogen-fixing plants like legumes, and vining plants like squashes or potatoes.

41

Biodegradable
Mandala Art

We know composting is good for the soil. We know creativity is goodfor our souls. Why not put those together by creating a biodegradable mandala? A mandala, meaning circle in ancient Sanskrit, is a form of geometric art made within a large circle. The creation of religious mandalas is a sacred practice in both Hindu and Buddhist cultures, as they represent both the ideal form of the Universe and the connection between the spiritual and physical worlds. They also represent the impermanence of life, as they are destroyed shortly after their creation.

Let's use the meditative, creative and connected practice of making a mandala and gifting it back to Nature to care for ourselves and the planet.

WHAT YOU NEED

Plant materials like cut flowers, twigs, petals, seed-pods, leaves and bark, etc.
Secateurs or scissors
A flat soil surface
A camera

1 Forage for your art materials on a walk or from your garden, or use cut flowers and greenery from bouquets about to be discarded.

2 Find a spot on the soil to create your mandala, preferably near or around a favourite tree or plant.

3 Begin by creating a large circle using your foraged materials. Then start to layer in more plant materials in geometric shapes and patterns. Create slowly and with focus and appreciation.

4 Take a photo of your final creation for posterity and leave all the materials as they are to biodegrade back into the soil.

....

REFLECTIONS

- *How did you feel as you conducted this practice? What did you notice inside your mind and body?*
- *How does gratitude for plants and Earth feel inside you?*

A MANDALA IS A FORM OF GEOMETRIC ART MADE WITHIN A LARGE CIRCLE.

Toxic-free Gardening

Regenerative agriculture prioritises growing food in ways that protect the health of the whole ecosystem, along with the health of the soil. One way is through natural fertilisation and toxic-free pest and weed control. In toxic-free gardening, compost, crop rotations and crop covers nourish the soil and fertilise the plants. Companion planting also nourishes the soil while deterring some unwanted insects and attracting other beneficial ones. By choosing more natural options, we avoid using toxic pesticides, herbicides and fertilisers in our own gardens and create safe havens for biodiversity to flourish, as well as safeguarding our health.

WHAT YOU NEED
Materials for naturally caring for your garden like organic fertilisers, compost, worm castings, neem oil and rubbing alcohol

....

1 First, check to see if the products you're already using contain toxins such as glyphosate (herbicide), pyrethroid (pesticide), metaldehyde (pesticide), methomyl (insecticide) or atrazine (herbicide) – if so, it's time for some new garden assistance.

2 Do your best to determine what your garden needs.

- Do you need to get rid of destructive caterpillars while calling in the helpful ones? Plant basil and dill near tomato plants to repel the hornworms and plant milkweed (*Asclepias*) around the edges of your garden to attract the monarchs.

- Do you need to rid your squash of powdery mildew? Mix your own solution of 1 tablespoon of bicarbonate of soda (baking soda) and ½ teaspoon of non-detergent soap with 4.5 litres (1 gallon) of water and spray all over the fronts and backs of leaves and stems.
- Do you want to call in the bees to pollinate or the ladybirds (ladybugs) to prey on aphids? Plant borage or let dandelions grow for the bees, and plant marigolds for the ladybirds.
- Create a solution of neem oil, non-detergent soap and water and spray liberally over your garden as a general pest repellant. This is best done during dawn or dusk to avoid disturbing pollinators.

3 Research new ways of nourishing the plants and soils in your garden by making compost teas, or banana peel waters, or sprinkling crushed eggshells in your garden (which also repels slugs).

4 Commend yourself for finding new collaborative and healthy ways to tend to the health of your garden, the Earth and your health, too.

....

REFLECTIONS

- *Where might you be allowing toxic thoughts, patterns, situations or people to pollute your life?*
- *What new, more supportive beliefs, thoughts and people can you encourage/invite into your life instead of the toxic ones?*

43

Bring in the Birds

Back in *Practice 14*, we discovered the calming influence birds have on our nervous systems and sense of well-being. We can thank the birds for the power of their presence, while also encouraging them to keep coming to our spaces by creating bird-friendly habitats around our homes and gardens.

WHAT YOU NEED

Bird feeders and bird food (such as bird seed, peanuts and fat balls)
Bird bath and/or bird boxes
Native trees and plants
Space to set up your gifts for the birds

1 Decide where you'd like to create some bird sanctuary spaces in your garden, and what you'd like to provide for the birds.

2 To attract a greater variety of birds, place bird feeders at different heights, with some closer to the ground, some at shrub height and some up in a tree.

3 If you don't have your own garden, you can also hang bird feeders in the branches of trees outside your home.

4 If you do have a garden, keep it a welcoming and safe space for the birds by planting native trees and plants and avoiding synthetic pesticides and herbicides. Don't forget to provide water for the birds to drink and bathe in and perhaps a bird box or two.

5 Be sure to clean out the bird feeders and bird baths every other week or so.

....

REFLECTION

- *How does it feel to observe a wild animal positively interact with a space you created?*

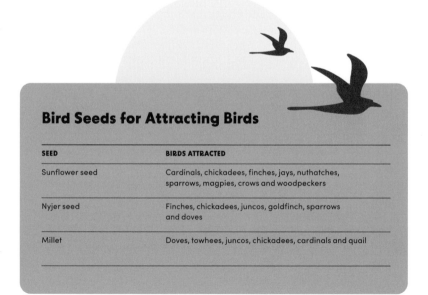

Bird Seeds for Attracting Birds

SEED	BIRDS ATTRACTED
Sunflower seed	Cardinals, chickadees, finches, jays, nuthatches, sparrows, magpies, crows and woodpeckers
Nyjer seed	Finches, chickadees, juncos, goldfinch, sparrows and doves
Millet	Doves, towhees, juncos, chickadees, cardinals and quail

Plant a Pollinator Garden

A healthy planet depends on pollinators, like bees, butterflies, moths, beetles, wasps, flies, bats and hummingbirds, for much of the food we eat. When we plant a pollinator garden, and garden with their health in mind, we recognise the service they provide and give back to them in return.

WHAT YOU NEED

Access to the internet for research

Outdoor space for planting

Potting compost (if planting pots and planters)

Pollinator-friendly plants for your region

1 Decide where to plant a pollinator garden or introduce pollinator-friendly plants to your existing garden. For example, bees love the herb borage and butterflies love echinacea and lavender. Keep in mind that sunny spots are important for butterflies, especially when drying their wings after first emerging from their chrysalis. If you don't have a garden, you can also plant native pollinator-friendly plants in pots or planters.

2 Research the types of plants that will attract pollinators. Plants native to your area are always great options – for example, in the USA, try growing asters and milkweed (*Asclepias syriaca*) – along with flowers that produce a lot of nectar like cosmos and lantana.

3 Gather and plant your pollinator-friendly plants. Water and care for them. Let these plants go to seed and allow their seeds to be dispersed by the winds to create more pollinator-friendly plants around your neighbourhood.

4 Avoid using any synthetic pesticides or herbicides in your garden.

Optional: If you have a large garden space, here are some more ways to create a butterfly- and pollinator-friendly habitat:

- Add a water feature for hydration.
- Plant flowering plants at different heights that bloom at different times.
- Place bare branches near caterpillar-friendly plants to create a safe space for them to hang onto during their chrysalis stage.
- Add some small rock piles near butterfly-friendly plants to create sheltering spaces for them to rest.

••

REFLECTIONS

- *Thinking about your life, how have you created a sense of safety and sanctuary for yourself?*
- *How have you created a safe space for Nature to thrive?*

Befriend Your Weeds

We're often taught that weeds are a nuisance, but they're actually powerful allies for our health and well-being. Take, for example, nettle and dandelion.

Nettle, with ragged-edged leaves infamous for their sting, is also known for nourishing our bodies. High in vitamins, minerals and antioxidants, it's strengthening and hydrating, and also soothes the skin and promotes the growth of hair and nails.

Dandelions, with their puffball seed heads and happy yellow flowers that bees adore, are probably one of the most common weeds across the world. Adaptable and resilient, able to grow through the cracks in concrete as easily as in your garden, dandelion leaves and roots make for powerful digestive tonics, while also supporting the liver and heart.

Let's pay attention to, and learn from, the weeds, flowers and herbs that are growing in abundance around our homes.

WHAT YOU NEED

Plant ID app for research
Fresh or dried weeds,
herbs or flowers that you connected with (optional)

··

1 Begin to notice the weeds and flowers that grow naturally along paths, roads, fields and gardens. Are you noticing a lot of dandelion blooms? Or is it clover that's catching your eye everywhere you go? Or maybe it's the dark green leaves of nettle that are drawing you in?

2 After identifying the natural plants, flowers and herbs showing up around you, look into their nutritional and medicinal uses. Is there any correlation to issues that may be going on in your life?

3 Continue to notice and identify the weeds, herbs and flowers that seem to draw your attention throughout the week and contemplate the lesson those plants have for you.

4 If you feel called to do so, drink a tea made from the plants showing up for you, either from plants harvested from clean sources around your home or from pre-packaged dried teas.

....

REFLECTION

- *What weeds showed up for you and what messages might they have for you?*

WEEDS CAN BE POWERFUL ALLIES FOR OUR HEALTH AND WELL-BEING.

Prune to Grow

Sometimes we need to let things go in order to make room for our own growth. Plants are the same: by pruning back and harvesting plants we actually spur on new growth within them.

Physically decluttering our home is a great example of letting things go, but what about when our clutter is emotional? How can we let go of something that feels negative and heavy yet intangible at the same time, like the negative feelings brought on by eco-anxiety? We can use a self-care exercise like this pruning practice to create a physical representation of what we are emotionally releasing.

When we mindfully prune a plant, we cut away more than branches, stems and leaves. We also create an opportunity to cut away and release thoughts, emotions and past situations that are no longer serving us.

So let's help our plants and ourselves thrive by pruning away the old.

WHAT YOU NEED

Garden shears and/or saw
(may be needed for pruning thick tree branches)
Gardening gloves (and other proper attire)
Plants or trees that need pruning

1 Determine which plant(s) and/or tree(s) in or around your home need a good pruning.

2 Research how your plant(s) prefer to be pruned in order to encourage more growth.

3 Gather your pruning equipment.

4 Set an intention for this practice by leaning into any thoughts, emotions or past situations you'd like to cut away.

5 Let the plant(s) know you'll be cutting them back in order to help them grow.

6 Start clipping off branches, stems and/or leaves. With each cut, imagine yourself cutting away an undesired thought, emotion or past issue. With each fall of a branch, stem or leaf, feel yourself letting go of what you no longer wish to carry.

7 When you have finished, take a moment to breathe deeply as you look appreciatively at all you cut away. Take another deep breath and notice how much lighter you feel.

8 Discard your clipped plant materials in your compost or garden waste bin.

....

REFLECTIONS

- *How did you feel at the start of this practice?*
- *How did you feel at the end of this practice?*

Give Thanks
to Water

Clean water is essential to life on Earth, yet too often we forget how valuable and precious it truly is. From drought to floods, ocean acidification to dead zones, pollution and wasteful usage to the plastic waste problem increased by bottled water, we humans must reimagine and transform our relationship with water. This begins with daily appreciation for the gift that is clean and drinkable water, and a commitment to give back to water in return.

1. From your first sip in the morning to your last gulp before bed, spend time each day feeling appreciation for the water you drink.

2. Take a moment to think about the journey of this water, from ocean to sky, to rain, to land and eventually to you. Feel grateful for all this water has been through before providing you with hydration.

3. Before bathing or washing up, conduct a similar gratitude practice, giving thanks to water and its ability to cleanse and purify.

4. Each day, allow yourself to deepen into appreciation and gratitude for the water you interact with. To do this, hold the feelings of gratitude within you for as long as you can, gently redirecting your thoughts back to thankfulness when your mind begins to wander.

5 Commit to one or two actions you can take to help protect and conserve water. Options include:

- Conscious and non-wasteful use of water.
- Removing or minimising your use of plastic water bottles.
- Creating a water tray for birds, bees and butterflies in your garden or on your porch.
- Harvesting rainwater for your plants and gardens using water butts attached to your gutters, or simply putting buckets out in the rain.
- Supporting those protecting Earth's oceans and fresh waters like the Indigenous-led Water Protector Legal Collective, the Pacific Institute, WaterAid and Project WET.

••

REFLECTIONS

- *How did this water gratitude practice influence your mental health?*
- *What is your commitment to protecting water?*

Clothes Swap

The clothing we wear impacts Earth's health and our health. The fast fashion industry is especially damaging – this refers to manufacturers who have moved toward cheaper, lower quality, mass production to keep up with changing trends. The dyes and materials they use are often toxic and synthetic. This significantly contributes to greenhouse gas emissions, environmental degradation and human rights violations. Thankfully, we can be a part of the solution through the way we shop for, or swap, our clothes.

....

HOW TO HOST A CLOTHES SWAP

1. Set a time and location and find at least three friends who are interested in joining in.

2. Ask each guest to go through their wardrobe, removing items they no longer wear or want, which are also clean and in good condition.

3. You can also ask your guests if they have any specific requests for types of clothing they are looking for or need.

4. Set up spaces for each person to display the clothes they brought and allow everyone to view the goods before commencing the swaps.

5 To make it even more fun, include some drinks and snacks either before or after the clothes swap.

6 Donate all items not claimed by the end of the party.

7 For those who can't (or don't want to) host a clothes swap, here are some options to avoid fast fashion and keep more of your money, too:

- Spend some time this week going through your wardrobe, removing any clothing you no longer want or wear. Donate and share these pieces however you see fit.
- Visit vintage, resale and charity shops to find unique items that match your style. You can also shop for vintage and resold clothes online, with websites like ThredUP.
- Instead of buying fancy outfits for special events you'll probably only wear once or twice, consider renting pieces from websites specialising in high-quality and fashionable options, like Rent the Runway.

**WE CAN BE A PART OF THE SOLUTION
THROUGH THE WAY WE SHOP FOR,
OR SWAP, OUR CLOTHES.**

49

Bring Your Own Reusables

Most plastics are made from fossil fuels and contain harmful chemicals. This has negative impacts on the health of the climate, wildlife and us, too. Additionally, single-use plastics (plastics used once and thrown away) are non-biodegradable, meaning they leach toxic chemicals into the surrounding environment as they slowly degrade into smaller pieces. These microscopic pieces of plastic then work their way into both the oceanic and terrestrial food webs. Unfortunately, much of this plastic pollution comes from our packaging.

When we take actions that we know have direct impacts on Earth's health and our health, we empower ourselves to be a part of the solution.

1 Begin by doing an audit of your single-use plastic. Where do you use the most plastic items and where might it be possible to switch to reusable options?

2 Think about ways you can swap in reusable options, for example:

- Carry your own reusable bags, water bottles, travel mugs and straws.
- Instead of using plastic water bottles, buy a reusable water bottle and water filter.
- Shop in bulk where possible and bring your own containers.
- Ask your favourite restaurants if you can bring in your own reusable containers for to-go orders or leftovers.
- Whenever possible, choose biodegradable disposable items made from paper, bamboo, corn or other plant fibres.

REFLECTIONS

- *How does reducing your plastic waste impact your relationship with Earth?*
- *How does reducing your plastic waste impact your relationship with yourself?*

Solutions to Single-Use Plastics

When used appropriately, plastic is a pretty amazing material for both its flexibility and durability. Unfortunately, much of the plastic currently produced and used on our planet is meant to be used once and then discarded. This is a reckless way to work with a nearly indestructible material; a material that takes hundreds of years to breakdown, while accumulating and leaching toxic chemicals as it does so. Unfortunately, the disposable culture that plastic packaging created is now the norm all over the globe. In order to truly solve the problem of plastic pollution, the manufacturing industry will have to replace oil-based plastics with more natural and biodegradable options, known as bioplastics.

These options already exist, such as:

- A non-toxic and fully biodegradable bioplastic made from the juice of the prickly pear cactus, created by researchers in Mexico.

- Shrilk, a completely biodegradable bioplastic made from a material called chitosan, which is found in the exoskeletons of crustaceans, blended with a protein from silk.

- PHA (Polyhydroxyalkanoates), a completely compostable plastic alternative made from bacterial fermentation.

- Packaging and plastic alternatives made from mushrooms and their web-like mycelium.

Please remember that there are many solutions available for our current plastic plague, and you are a part of that solution.

Go on a Clean-up Walk

Walking in Nature benefits us by relaxing our nervous systems, boosting our immunity and expanding our perspectives. Unfortunately, we also know that human rubbish currently litters the planet, so it's likely we'll experience some of this on our walks. By taking time to pick up litter and dispose of it properly, we give our thanks to Earth for all she provides.

Let's dedicate some of our walks to Earth by cleaning up litter we find along our way.

WHAT YOU NEED
Rubbish bag
Glove(s)
Hand sanitiser

1. Decide on your walking route and gather your materials.
2. Set the intention to look out for, and properly dispose of, litter seen on your walk.
3. Conduct a walk at least three times throughout the week.
4. Report any items that are too big or hazardous to dispose of on your own.

If you don't feel comfortable conducting a clean-up of your own, why not volunteer for community clean-up projects within your area? If you're feeling really inspired, you can also organise a community clean-up to beautify an area in your neighbourhood.

REFLECTIONS

- *How do you feel after completing these clean-up walks?*
- *How can you commit to cleaning up and leaving Nature better than you found her?*

Dedicate some of your walks to Earth by cleaning up litter you find along your way.

51

Create Wildflower Seed Bombs

Believe it or not, lawns pose big problems for our planet. Manicured lawns are a problem because they are high maintenance, sometimes need treating with chemicals, and require watering, which puts a strain on precious water resources (especially in arid regions). Cultivated lawns also suppress the growth of wild plants and wildflowers, which are vital for nourishing the soil, along with numerous animal species such as birds and pollinators.

Wildflowers require much less water and maintenance, while also providing important food and habitats for beneficial animals. Thankfully, you don't need a whole lawn to share the wildflower love, you just need a place to plant (whether that be in a pot or in the ground), some soil, seeds, sun and water.

Wildflower seed bombs are little balls of seeds mixed with a growth medium. They can be thrown anywhere there is soil and are satisfying to both make and sow.

WHAT YOU NEED
Wildflower seeds (native to your region)
Pieces of construction paper, or recycled paper or some newspaper
Food processor or hand-held blender
A small bowl
A large mixing bowl
Potting compost or soil

••

1 Determine where you want to plant your wildflowers, whether that be in your garden or a planter.

2 Research wildflower species native to your area and how to get hold of their seeds. Avoid using the seeds of invasive species.

3 Here's how to make your wildflower seed bombs:

- Cut or tear the paper into strips. Place those strips in the small bowl and cover with water. Let the strips soak for about 25 minutes.
- Drain and squeeze the water from the paper, then add the wet paper to a food processer, or use a hand-held blender to turn the wet paper into a kind of paste.
- Transfer the wet paper paste to the large mixing bowl, then sprinkle in your wildflower seeds. Add small amounts of potting compost or soil and then mix well.
- Shape the mixture into small balls. If the mixture is too dry, sprinkle in some more water. If the mixture is too wet, add a little more potting compost or soil.
- Once shaped, allow to dry and harden for 24–48 hours.

4 Once the seed balls are dry, plant by throwing them into bare corners of your garden, into planters filled with some potting compost, or into bare spots in your neighbourhood.

....

REFLECTION

- *How are you nourishing that which nourishes you?*

"IN NATURE, NOTHING EXISTS ALONE." – RACHEL CARSON

52

Radically Accept This Moment

A wise Buddhist adage states:

'PAIN IS INEVITABLE. SUFFERING IS OPTIONAL.'

We feel both pain and suffering regarding our current relationship with Earth. The pain of environmental destruction is inevitable, yet eco-anxiety only heightens our suffering.

One way we learn to opt out of suffering is through radical acceptance of what is. Acceptance of the situation we're in and acceptance that we humans are the cause of our challenges, but can also find the solutions.

Radical acceptance does not mean approval, nor does it mean surrendering our goals. Radical acceptance means releasing our resistance and accepting the reality in front of us. When we accept that some things are out of our control, we release fear, guilt, shame and more. We also free up energy to devote to acting where we can. When we accept what is, it becomes easier to accept what must be done to deal with this.

Radical acceptance is self-care.

Let's stay open-hearted with a final self-care practice that encourages radical acceptance of our environmental challenges and solutions.

WHAT YOU NEED
Your journal and pen
Time and space for inner reflection

....

1 Observe your inner landscape – how are you currently questioning or resisting the truth around Earth's health?

2 Remember that while these problems exist, you alone cannot solve them, yet your actions always make a difference.

3 Remind yourself that we know both the causes of our environmental problems along with their solutions.

4 As you think about the problems, allow yourself to feel whatever you feel, whether that be fear, anger, sadness, guilt or grief. Breathe deeply and intentionally through the discomfort of this acceptance. Notice and attend to the sensations you feel in your body (you can use the somatic practices shared in *Practices 2–5* to move these emotions through your body).

5 As you think about solutions and your own actions, allow yourself to feel hope, possibility, curiosity, cooperation, support, expansion and love arise within you. Lean into the sensations of these pleasurable feelings to help them grow.

6 Acknowledge the transformative ability to find pleasure in life even when experiencing pain.

7 Make a list of actions you're already taking and will take, to support the health of Earth, including many of the practices already shared within these pages.

8 Take a moment to appreciate yourself and the millions of other people caring and acting for Earth, biodiversity and each other. Remember you're never truly alone on this interconnected, living planet.

....

REFLECTIONS

- *What does it feel like to accept and believe in the possibility of a better future?*
- *What does a future that prioritises planetary health look and feel like to you?*

'Knowing that you love
the Earth changes you,
activates you to defend
and protect and celebrate.
But when you feel that
the Earth loves you
in return, that feeling
transforms the relationship
from a one-way street
into a sacred bond.'

– Robin Wall Kimmerer

Congratulations for remembering your sacred bond with Earth.

Congratulations for loving Earth and knowing you are loved by her in return.

It's this love that guides us forward into a world of solutions.

Conclusion:
Rooted in Love

It's time to transform our relationship with Earth as an act of collective self-care, because our health is interconnected with Earth's health.

It's time to accept that our future on Earth will be different from our past and present, and that we must adapt to survive and thrive. It's time to accept that our adaptations must include taking care of each other and the living planet we call home.

It's time to understand that we are living through environmental catastrophes as a vital lesson in interconnectivity and love.

No single person can solve the environmental challenges we face, yet each of us can cultivate our interconnection and care for Nature. Each of us can remember and accept that we are Nature, too.

We already possess everything we need to improve our relationship with Earth. We know how to generate clean energy, make biodegradable packaging, protect the waters, regenerate the soils, prioritise biodiversity and reforest the land. We have the wisdom, technology, innovation and collective desire to create, consume and live in collaborative, life-affirming ways.

It's not too late for us to change. It's not too late to prioritise interconnectivity over profits. In fact, each of us is actively co-creating that world right now, through intentional love-fuelled actions we take for Earth, each other and ourselves. Actions like those found within this book.

Throughout these pages, we've used our relationship with Nature for self-care, connected with Nature's emotional and creative support, grown our gratitude and given back to Earth.

By caring for ourselves and Earth simultaneously, we've remembered our reciprocal love.

It is this rooted love, not fear, that will keep us connecting, creating with, and giving back daily, in ways that will transform Earth and ourselves for the better.

It's time for change, and that change begins with us.

About
the Author

Rachael Cohen is a Nature-based spiritual life coach, plant connector and author. When her experiences as an environmental educator, wild animal specialist and mother left her anxious and distraught over society's destruction of Nature, Rachael cultivated a creative relationship with plants that transformed her life. She founded *Infinite Succulent*, specialising in plant art connections, and *Our Infinite Nature*, for facilitating and growing our spiritual connections with nature.

Rachael can frequently be found connecting with her husband, two daughters and snuggly dog on hikes, in hammocks or over herbal tea.

Rachael is also the author of *Everyday Plant Magic: Change your Life through the Magical Energy of Nature* (Hardie Grant, 2022) and *Infinite Succulent: Miniature Art to Keep or Share* (Countryman Press, 2019).

To learn more, please visit OurInfiniteNature.co.

Acknowledgements

Thank you to you, the readers of this book, and all who care deeply for the health of Mother Earth and those who live upon her. Thank you for remembering our interconnection and thank you for caring about, believing in and acting for a more sustainable future.

Thank you to everyone working towards protecting and conserving Earth and her natural resources. Thank you to the connectors and protectors of the land, the water, the air and the soil. Thank you to all currently envisioning, designing, developing, implementing and creating the solutions to our current environmental challenges. Thank you to those who connect with Nature and help others do the same.

Thank you to my editor Kate Burkett and the entire publishing team over at Hardie Grant. You saw the need and potential for this book, and trusted me to write it, and for that I am so grateful.

Thank you to my agent Tisha Morris, who I'm equally honoured to call a mentor and friend.

Thank you to my daughters, A & Z, for your curiosity, imagination and kindness.

Thank you to all the children of the world, for the constant reminder that we are worth saving.

Thank you to my husband, for the constant unconditional love and support and for understanding my nocturnal habits when in book-writing mode.

And thank you to some of my greatest teachers, the trees, who constantly guide me to look at the world from an interconnected perspective.

References & Resources/
Further Reading

Arvay, Clemens G. *The Biophilia Effect: A Scientific and Spiritual Exploration of the Healing Bond Between Humans and Nature.* Sounds True, 2018.

(Edited by) Buzzell, Linda and Chalquist, Craig. *Ecotherapy: Healing with Nature in Mind.* Counterpoint Publishing, California, 2009.

Cameron, Julia. *The Artist's Way: A Spiritual Path to Higher Creativity.* TarcherPerigee, 1992.

Cohen, Rachael. *Everyday Plant Magic: Change Your Life Through the Magical Energy of Nature.* Hardie Grant, 2022.

Cohen, Rachael. *Infinite Succulent: Miniature Living Art to Keep or Share.* Countryman Press, 2019.

Failla, Maria. *Growing Joy: The Plant Lover's Guide to Cultivating Happiness (and Plants).* St. Martin's Publishing Group, 2022.

Johnson, Ayana Elizabeth and Wilkinson, Katherine K. *All We Can Save: Truth, Courage and Solutions for the Climate Crisis.* One World, 2020.

Kimmerer, Robin Wall. *Braiding Sweetgrass: Indigenous Wisdom, Scientific Knowledge and the Teachings of Plants.* Milkweed Editions, 2015.

Laws, John Muir and Lygren, Emilie. *How to Teach Nature Journaling: Curiosity, Wonder, Attention.* Heydey, 2020.

Loewe, Emma. *Return to Nature: The New Science of How Natural Landscapes Restore Us.* Harper One, New York, 2022.

Li, Dr. Qing. *Forest Bathing: How Trees Can Help You Find Health and Happiness.* Penguin Life, 2018.

Plevin, Julia. *The Healing Magic of Forest Bathing: Finding Calm, Creativity and Connection in the Natural World.* Ten Speed Press, 2018.

Rawlins, Vicki. *The Power of Flowers: Turning Pieces of Mother Nature into Transformative Works of Art.* Quarto Publishing Group, 2022.

Shealy, Norman (M.D., Ph.D.). *The Illustrated Encyclopedia of Healing Remedies.* Harper Collins Publishers, 2018.

Simard, Suzanne. *Finding the Mother Tree: Discovering the Wisdom of the Forest.* Vintage, 2021.

VanZile, Jon. *Houseplants for a Healthy Home.* Adams Media, 2018.

Wardley, Tessa. *The Eco Hero Handbook: Simple Solutions to Tackle Eco-anxiety.* Ivy Press, 2021.

Watts, Tammah. *Keep Looking Up: Your Guide to the Powerful Healing of Birdwatching.* Hay House Inc., 2023.

White, Heather. *One Green Thing: Discover Your Hidden Power to Help Save the Planet.* Harper Horizon, 2022.

Index

Published in 2024 by Hardie Grant Books,
an imprint of Hardie Grant Publishing

Hardie Grant Books (London)
5th & 6th Floors
52–54 Southwark Street
London SE1 1UN

Hardie Grant Books (Melbourne)
Building 1, 658 Church Street
Richmond, Victoria 3121

hardiegrantbooks.com

British Library Cataloguing-in-Publication
Data. A catalogue record for this book
is available from the British Library.

Self-care for Eco-anxiety

ISBN: 9781784887353

Publishing Director: Kajal Mistry
Senior Commissioning Editor: Kate Burkett
Design: Claire Warner Studio
Copy Editor: Emily Rogers
Proofreader: Caroline West
Indexer: Cathy Heath
Production Controller: Gary Hayes

Colour Reproduction by p2d

Printed and bound in China
by Leo Paper Products Ltd

Please note that none of the self-care
practices shared in this book should be
considered to be providing or replacing
medical advice. Please consult with your
healthcare providers before taking any
new herbal supplements, especially
if you have prior medical conditions.
If you are struggling with your mental
health, please reach out for support.

MIX
Paper | Supporting
responsible forestry
FSC™ C020056